NATURE'S TERRORIST

HURRICANE IRMA

*The Unleashing of an Unstoppable Fury
on the tiny Island of Anguilla in the Caribbean*

D0839460

Nature's Terrorist Hurricane Irma
– The Unleashing of an Unstoppable Fury on the Tiny Island of Anguilla in the Caribbean
Copyright © 2018 J. Christopher Richardson

FIRST EDITION PRINTING
Visit the author's website at:
www.rpgtc.net

Paperback ISBN: 978-0-9970234-2-8

Written by: J. Christopher Richardson | consultchris4@gmail.com

Edited by: Charlie and Lyn Dubois

Cover Design & Formatting by: Eli Blyden | www.EliTheBookGuy.com

Library of Congress Cataloging-in-Publication Data:
An application to register this book for cataloging has been submitted to the Library of Congress.

Printed in the United States of America by: A&A Printing | www.PrintShopCentral.com

DEDICATION

I dedicate this piece of literature to my father, Morgan Richardson, who was born and raised in Anguilla. As a former police officer and Keeper of Prisons, he has impacted many lives. Whilst my mother, Enid Richardson, was an educator, it was my dad who taught my siblings and me the sounds of the letters of the alphabet and got us on the path of reading.

Nature's Terrorist Hurricane Irma

ACKNOWLEDGMENTS

I wish to thank the many persons who have assisted me along the journey of completing my second book.

Charlie and Lynn DuBois are great friends of mine whom I met as guests few years ago at one of Anguilla's five-star properties for which I worked. During the storm I heard a click on my phone and on opening it I saw a very kind message from them and at the end they wrote, "Write a story on the storm and we will be your chief proofreaders." I was well aware of their professions and was humbled by their gesture. They were true to their word. Thanks for your patience; you stood by me through my periods of writing blocks and laziness.

Thanks to Marshall Karp, who wrote *Lomax and Biggs* mystery novels, as well as the *NYPD Red* series of novels under the James Patterson label. His encouragement, support and sound advice were invaluable. Just before the storm he sent me a text that read, "Chris, safe journey through the storm and please write the story; I can't wait to read it."

I acknowledge all others, including my wife, Sandra, my children and grandchildren, who permitted me the necessary time away to dedicate to this exercise.

I give thanks to God Almighty, whose sustaining power has been at the forefront of every step that I take.

CONTENTS

FOREWORD

When we are outside and the sun warms our faces, we think of Anguilla and our wonderful times there. We reminisce about the Anguillians we have come to know as friends. To think of the Terrorist, Hurricane Irma, and the destruction of the island is heartbreaking. The sudden loss of jobs and income security, homes and everyday routines is unimaginable. But, more than the loss of a paradise, we think of the awful way Irma changed the lives of people we care for deeply.

In September, 2017, as the storm bore down on Anguilla, we reached out to Chris Richardson with wishes for his safety and that of his family. And, knowing Chris as an exceptional storyteller by reading his memoir, *Looking Back: Through the Eyes of a Teacher's Son*, we suggested he chronicle the hurricane and the island's recovery.

We met Chris years ago on our first visit to the Cuisinart Golf Resort and Spa, where he was a lead executive. Over the years, our talks with him and notes over the internet have been more than pleasant exchanges, they've been conversations filled with humor and insight into an island we've come to love above all others in the Caribbean. We came to know Chris as a skilled manager, a caring family man, a proud Anguillian, and an author with a voice that is both honest and true. We are certain that our experience has been shared by many guests of the properties Chris has helped manage.

In this book you will find a vivid account of the harrowing hours when Irma terrorized Anguilla and of the heroic days when Anguillians rose to rebuild and renew. On these pages are tales of sadness and humor, of missteps and shortsightedness, of compassion and bravery, but, above all, of enduring faith and the will to endure.

We are honored to have contributed in some small way to the completion of *Nature's Terrorist Hurricane Irma* and know you will come away from reading it with a deeper understanding of Anguilla, of the proud people who make it their home and how their lives were forever changed.

– Charles and Lynn DuBois

NATURE'S TERRORIST

HURRICANE IRMA

*The Unleashing of an Unstoppable Fury
on the tiny Island of Anguilla in the Caribbean*

by Chris RICHARDSON

Nature's Terrorist Hurricane Irma

INTRODUCTION

I was born and raised till the age of 13 years in a village called Sandy Point on the island of St. Kitts, from which I have gleaned many stories that have shaped my thinking.

During my primary school years, one of my teachers shared a story about a deer and a turtle. The story was spawned by the class' refusal to comply to her request. She had placed a mathematical problem on the blackboard and asked that all students solve the problem but hadn't taught us how.

The upstart that I was, I asked all the students to join me in protesting against her wishes by closing our exercise books and placing our writing pencils diagonally across them. After five minutes of the teacher's walking about in wait for us to complete the problem, she realized the class was adamant that it would not even attempt the question.

She was quite annoyed and inquired as to why there were no attempts, and I stood to my classmates' defense. I told her it was unfair for her to give the class a problem and not to have provided a step-by-step method to complete it. At that point, she placed her hand on her hip and began detailing a story about a deer and a land turtle.

She told the class to face the mountain, Mount Liamuigua, look at it for the remainder of the lesson period of fifteen minutes with no talking, and then write five words that best described it. All thirty students described its size. As our vocabulary was limited as ten-year-old children, the words we used included: high, tall, big, huge, fat. The teacher, after having us read our answers, responded with a smile of disgust, "Children, what about the beauty of the mountain? How about describing the greenery spotted by volcanic rocks?"

Our teacher went on a discourse and explained, "One day a deer challenged a land turtle that its movements were so slow that it would never be able to climb Mount Liamuigua. The deer told the turtle that the mountain was too high for it to cross over. But the turtle told the deer it sees a plateau, not a mountain. The deer told the land turtle it was the dumbest thought to envision the mountain as plateau and with the height of the mountain, only a giraffe can climb over it. The turtle started the journey maintaining it was a plateau, while the deer packed a bag of goodies and decided to go ahead of the turtle. After that, they never saw each other for a few years. One day the deer decided to take a walk on the other side of the mountain, remembering its unsuccessful attempt to cross over the same mountain ahead of the turtle a few years earlier. Whilst taking a walk the deer saw the turtle making its last step to meet the foot of the other side of the mountain. The deer questioned the turtle as to how come it made it over while the deer had never been able to do so for the years it had been trying. The turtle simply replied, 'You saw a mountain but I saw a plateau, and indeed it was a plateau.'"

The moral of that story relative to the optimism of that turtle never escaped me. It was, moreover, reinforced when in 2012 I was introduced to the book *Positive Intelligence* written by Shirzad Chamine, who noted only 20 percent of teams and individuals achieve their true potential. Two forces operate within the human mind: Sabotage and Sage. The

Sabotage is as its name suggests. It's our ultimate enemy. On the other hand is the Sage, which is our friend. These two elements war within our minds and our overcoming power depends on our choice as to the muscle we wish to exercise; the Sage muscle or the Sabotage muscle.

The story of Hurricane Irma, the Terrorist, is a piece of literature illustrating Anguilla's defeat and triumph. How does one go through a storm and rebound within a reasonable period? Where is our focus? Is it on the problem or the solution?

In the immediate aftermath of the storm, one of my colleagues lost her job and fell ill. Having lost her job, she lost her medical insurance coverage. On seeking medical care, she was diagnosed with cancer. Fear gripped her as she had a baby only months old and was a mother of three. She is currently undergoing chemotherapy and two things that touch me every time I visit her is her level of optimism and her faith. Her positive attitude is reminiscent of the land turtle's determination to beat the odds and climb over the mountain.

There is no mountain that is insurmountable. Some may wish to run over, while others may only have the potential to crawl like the land turtle. Whatever your potential, exercise it! Never succumb to the perplexities of life, be an overcomer.

Nature's Terrorist Hurricane Irma

CHAPTER I

THE 9/11 "VICTIM"

In March of 2002, as the food and beverage manager of Malliouhana Hotel, I was tasked with the duty of welcoming a guest, a function that was customarily performed by the general manager/owner. He had called me earlier in the day and asked that I fill in for him as he wished to retire to his room earlier than usual on that particular day. The solid oak finished front desk was a literal "step down" from the porte cochere, the guest pick-up and drop-off point.

As I stood at the front desk in a professional manner in anticipation of receiving the guest, I was awestruck by this tall, wiry, ginger-haired and blue-eyed gentleman emerging from the taxi's rear seat. The car was driven by Walter, one of Anguilla's most gregarious taxi drivers. Walter's car was not the newest of the fleet of taxis and often would have been rejected on first sight by a reasonable thinking traveler; it defied all niceties and welcome jingles for the discerning traveler. Tash, the bellman who was an inch or two over five feet, was dwarfed by the guest as he opened the car door to offer the gentleman porter assistance. With a welcoming smile, Tash happily welcomed the guest but received no response. Nonetheless, Tash escorted him toward the front desk and pointed him to my presence to receive his official welcome from the resort's management.

As a trained hospitality practitioner for almost twelve years at that time, I had become accustomed to the snobbish behavior of a few guests, particularly those staying at five-star-rated resorts like Malliouhana Hotel; hence, I had no ego to be shattered. As the guest approached the desk on the instructions of the bellman, I stepped towards him with an extended hand of greeting and he responded by staring into my eyes with clenched teeth and a gaunt face. While my handshake of welcome was obviously ignored I continued and verbalized my welcome. My lessons on emotional intelligence took center stage at this point and I asked with concern, "Do you have all your luggage? I trust you had an uneventful flight." He remained mute, took his registration form from the front desk agent and ignored her instructions on completing it. He merely reached into his shirt pocket and pulled out a rustic, bent Faber tip pen and signed the registration card.

He allowed the agent to take the lead as he was escorted to his room, a junior suite which sat on the bluff overlooking a small beach called Turtle Cove. Although Anguilla has no private beaches, we often referred to Turtle Cove as a "semi-private beach," giving a little romantic flare to its exclusiveness; it was accessible only by way of entering the resort and could not be accessed from the Meads Bay beach which it bordered. When the agent returned, I questioned her as to the demeanor of the guest and at that point she said, "Chris, he is going to be a problem and he will be your project for the next ten days." Evidently, they all knew that it was my modus operandi to view challenges as opportunities and I was all excited to alert the entire team that we had had a "Special Attention Guest," noting the room number and the attitude that qualified him for this category.

For the first few days of his stay I thought the guest was mentally deranged; he visited neither the restaurants nor the bars. On perusing his room folio on the third day it was obvious he had not dined using any of the resort's dining options. Alarmingly, he had not left the property at any time in search for any meals. I reported it to the general manager who raised the suspicion that he might have come to the Caribbean to die, which I quickly dismissed. In the resort's morning executive meetings, he became the subject of discussion, and all fingers were pointing at me to ensure this guest did not hurt himself. Indeed, there were times I thought he was suicidal, particularly when I observed on the sixth day of his stay he had not removed any water from the mini bar. My personal amateur forensics revealed the shower was unused, as all the toweling and bathroom amenities remained untouched and no water residue was observed in either the tub, shower or face basin.

On the seventh day of his stay, I withdrew myself from the normal routine of my work duties, which at times were mundane and lacked excitement, and focused my attention on studying the unusual behavior pattern of this guest. Routinely, he walked to the Meads Bay beach bordering another hotel at five o'clock in the evening and for approximately one hour he would stare at the water and at intervals would throw pebbles into the sea, like a child in anger. On the ninth day, I decided to approach him and inquire as to the purpose of his visit and if the resort was meeting his expectations. Deep within I felt sorry that I had asked the questions as he turned his face robotically towards me with a blank expression and stared deeply into my eyes, inviting me to read his mind by way of his body language and kinesics. While I do consider myself as having a high emotional intelligence quotient, I was lost at interpreting the meaning of this guest's behavior. He soon walked away from me with a disposition of disgust and bitterness; at that point I said, "I trust all is well with the family." On hearing my comment, he halted his strides and, with his back turned to me, he exclaimed, "You don't know what it is like to have your entire family wiped out by some dammed terrorist and you are here asking me about my family! The World Trade Center came tumbling down with my wife and daughter; all I had in this world. Tell me, how do I go on?" For a moment I thought the comments I was hearing were a mere figment of my imagination or that I was actually daydreaming. I became dumbfounded and tried to imagine or recreate the 9/11 event in my mind; but I am sure my finite mind failed at creating the impact this despicable act would have had on the survivors or the families of the victims.

I have always been considered a man of many words but I just could not find the correct words to respond to his comments. After a few minutes of silence and staring at each other I responded cautiously, "I understand!" His blue eyes widened as he placed his hands on his hips. Speaking through his clenched teeth, which seemingly were discolored by the cigarettes that he substituted for his meals, he said, "What the hell do you know about understanding my situation; have you ever experienced such pain?" With tears trickling down his cheeks he exclaimed, "I wish to God it was me who would have died! It was blamed on terrorism but I don't know what to believe. All I know is I have absolutely no one in this world; actually, I am a dead man on earth, having no purpose or will to carry on."

The conversation was very sobering and it caused me to seriously ponder on those countries that are not accustomed to the peace that we in the western world know. I thought about the tribal wars, religious wars and political fighting that take place in some of the eastern countries with no intermittent peace, and I reminisced on the fact that we are blessed in so many ways.

The morning before he departed I positioned myself to bid him farewell. His steps were brisk but his facial expression remained as when he arrived, repulsive. He requested the same taxi cab he used for his arrival.

I stood a few feet away from him, anticipating his non-responsiveness to my farewell. I was quite poised as he looked in my direction; I guess it was his turn to read my thoughts and he did a good job at it. He stepped towards me and stated emphatically, "When you are under attack and you do not have the capacity or will power to respond, what do you do? When you are under a terror attack and you have nowhere to run or any place to hide, what do you do? When everything you have built over the years melts from before your very eyes like butter before the sun in mid-summer, how the hell will you respond? Losing my wife and daughter was all I had in this world and they were erased from mother's earth by the hands of some terrorist. Yes! I lost them all. How do I find my way in life?"

As he turned his back to me he settled his folio, and without any form of pleasantries he stepped to the cab; in sympathy I tried to imagine his pain and gently said to him, "Be strong, you will survive."

I did not realize that approximately sixteen years later I would reflect on this pain and hurt of this gentleman. It happened while I held onto a door on the early morning on or around 4:30 a.m. of September, 6th, 2017 in an effort to save my family's life from Irma, the Terrorist. Yes! The words of

Brian, the guest, resonated during that early morning of fear, anxiety, anguish and disbelief.

While I did not experience the horror of airplanes crashing into buildings as what happened on that fateful morning of 9/11, the passage of nature's Terrorist Hurricane Irma, caused me to reflect on the pain of a terror attack on my home and my dear island of Anguilla.

Nature's Terrorist Hurricane Irma

CHAPTER II

AN ECONOMY HINGED ON TOURISM

nguilla is an overseas British Territory and is the most northerly of the Leeward Islands. It boasts of a small population of approximately 13,900 occupying a land mass of thirty-five square miles; the island is sixteen miles long and three miles wide at its widest point. Anguilla is unique among most of the islands in the Caribbean as the majority of the land is owned by the natives and the islanders are very protective of their lands.

With the advent of tourism on the island in the early 1980s, some of the land is in alien hands but on a miniscule scale. Some of the major hotels sit on lands leased either from local families or the government.

Prior to the 1970s there had been a mass exodus of the natives in search of work on other Caribbean islands including St. Kitts (the island which governed Anguilla constitutionally until 1983) and the Dominican Republic. Some ventured as far as the United Kingdom in the early 1900s with most settling in Slough, England; hence the latter is referenced as "Little Anguilla."

During the early years, the natives who remained on island survived on subsistence farming and remittances from families, relatives and friends from overseas. However, it is important to interject that one of the commonalities among the Anguillians of the day was that of ensuring they had a roof over their heads; they sought to build their own houses. As finances were limited at the time, with minimal banking assistance available, the houses took extremely long periods to build; in rare cases, work begun on houses in the '70s may still be incomplete. More recently, with the advent of the indigenous banks (Caribbean Commercial

Bank and National Bank of Anguilla) significant funding became available to Anguillians. However, these sources collapsed with the global financial meltdown.

Our virgin beaches were used by the natives on rare occasions. They may have been used for an occasional beach party or quick swim. We, as natives, also used the beach for medicinal purposes. As children with head colds, it was common for our parents to bring us to the sea to take a few dives. A few moments after this exercise it was usual for one to observe mucus flowing from our nostrils. Never in our wildest dreams did we think at some point in time we would graciously share the thrills of beach time with our guests and it would constitute the ultimate economic engine of our country.

Prior to the 1980s, there were guest houses like Lloyd's Guest House, Rendezvous Bay Hotel and Yellow Banana Guest House, two of which sat on the interior of the island with the other in close proximity to one of Anguilla's finest beaches. But, at the turn of the 1980s we were about to embrace a different type of tourism. The Hauser family constructed Cinnamon Reef Hotel at Little Habour, bringing foreign investment into the island. Alongside this property was the Mariners Hotel at Sandy Ground, just a few steps away from the main cargo seaport and Cul de Sac at Rendezvous. These properties, except Lloyd's Guest House and Rendezvous Bay Hotel, have since ceased to exist as they both succumbed to the financial stresses of the day. However, these properties played key roles in the development of tourism that was soon to give way to upscale tourism in Anguilla. They were the main private sector employers and functioned as good corporate citizens. Short courses were conducted under the auspices of the Tourism Department in conjunction with other stakeholders. The courses were short, with durations of one to five days, but very meaningful for entry-level positions in the hospitality industry.

The flagship resort, Malliouhana Hotel, owned by British tycoon Leon Roydon, opened its doors for business as Anguilla's first five-star property in 1984. This property, which grew to a fifty-three room hotel perched on a bluff at Meads Bays, raised the bar for quality service delivery on the island. I recall once in one of our executive meetings in the conference room, Mr. Roydon made it clear to all of us, as members of the executive team, "I did not create this property for the chief executive officer or the president and his secretary; there must be another house for the secretary." At the time I was appalled as this was clearly discrimination and I challenged his affirmation. However, I soon realized there was such a concept known as positive discrimination. He was true to his statement on launching the property. The design and flair of the property attracted the famous and wealthy figures of the day.

The furnishings of this property were quite exquisite and the room rates and menu prices definitely matched the guests' purses. Paying fifty dollars for a shot of Hennessy XO was received without the "bat of an eye." Malliouhana attracted guests from all over the world. There was a guest who celebrated his birthday in 1988 and, as it was his fiftieth birthday, he was adamant on spending $50,000 over a five-day period. At the end of his stay the board and lodging cost fell way short of his target figure, so he distributed the remainder in tips to the front-line staff. Whilst this quantum of tipping was an isolated case, upscale tourism brought with it high service charges and heavy tippers. It was not uncommon for staff to receive $500 in tips from a single guest. As a matter of fact, I had witnessed guests giving a single staff member $1,500 in tips. It was common for guests to provide staff members state-of-the-art laptops and Androids. This type of reward caused many to adopt this industry as a means of their livelihood. The staff was not frazzled about the miniscule hourly wages offered by the employers; they focused on the service charge and the tips.

Later, in 1988, Cap Juluca came on stream as another five-star resort, followed by CuisinArt Resort and Spa (now renamed CuisinArt Golf Resort and Spa) in 1999, Viceroy Resort and Residencies (now renamed Four Seasons Resort and Residences) in 2010 and Zemi Beach Hotel and Spa in 2016. These resorts, including Malliouhana, are the biggest private-sector employers, with CuisinArt Golf Resort and Spa and Four Seasons Resorts and Residences alone employing over 1,500 of Anguilla's working population. It is estimated that close to 2,000 persons are employed directly in the tourism industry of Anguilla.

The industry has definitely brought a better way of life to many Anguillians and expatriates alike. It has led to many natives building their own homes with borrowed monies and making investments for themselves.

The global financial meltdown of 2008 dealt Anguilla's economy a blow. The island had experienced an economic boom between years 2005 and 2008. Two major construction projects came on stream and the construction sector saw its glory days during this period. Anguilla was in a position to state categorically that it had full employment. The lending institutions on the island, more so our indigenous banks, were quite optimistic about the island's economic future and granted loans with seeming impunity. The increased employment opportunities of the island led to an influx of expatriates from the Caribbean region and internationally. Hence, there was a shortage in the housing sector and natives were encouraged to build houses for rental purposes. Having the lands, many did not borrow from the banks discretionarily and would soon be left with buildings without tenants as the economy came tumbling down. The government of the day did feather its nest and that of the civil service, giving increases that would soon become unsustainable. The entire economy went into a tail-spin and prospects for recovery seemed dismal.

The two indigenous banks were left to collect on loans that were under-collateralized, allowing the number of underperforming loans to reach an all-time high of almost fifty percent. Ultimately, the banks were no longer able to survive such economic stresses.

With the financial global meltdown, the tourism industry was significantly adversely affected. Properties that once enjoyed occupancies of seventy to seventy-eight percent per annum plummeted to thirty-five and forty percent per annum. The huge spenders who would have otherwise chosen Anguilla as their preferred destination shied away, citing the island as too pricy. Most of the properties limped along and some went into disrepair, which worsened their business. By the time the world economy began to revive, some of the properties had lost their five-star acumen. The guests wanted value for their dollar and the products were just not up to par. The service charge and the tips dipped to the lowest ebb, leaving the natives in a socioeconomic quandary.

The hardship became evident, and compounding the situation, or, according to an island's idiom, "pouring salt in wounds," the government introduced taxes on an economy that was in need of resuscitation. The mother country, the United Kingdom, cited those handling our purse strings as lacking frugal sense and determined that it would not provide any financial assistance to alleviate the country's financial burden.

We had to "paddle our own canoe" as best we could with our famished resources. There had been the self-proclaimed pundits who made declarations that Anguilla's road to recovery would be a long and arduous one. However, the nationals had been hopeful for a brighter day and expected the changes in government to have been the panacea;

those with strong religious leniencies chose to be prayerful as they decried the statement of the German philosopher and economist Karl Marx, who stated that religion is the opiate of the masses.

CHAPTER III

TALES OF YESTERYEAR

Prior to the hurricane season, which begins annually in the month of June, the weather pundits did not hesitate to forecast that the 2017 season would be the most active in the history of such seasons. Like many of Anguilla's residents, I turned a deaf ear and was rather critical of such predictions. The touting of the effects of global warming had been continually addressed by world-renowned scientists to the disbelief of many; particular the newly elected president of the United States of America, Donald Trump, who opined it a mere figment of man's imagination, or a hoax.

Anguilla has been known to have received quite a few hurricanes. However, very little had been spoken of the hurricanes of 1950 and 1955. As we grew up, our parents only spoke about that horrible hurricane which was referenced as Donna Gale.

The devastation of Hurricane Donna, which struck the Lesser Antilles, including Anguilla, on September 4th, 1960, was viewed as a tale of the past as we intently listened to our parents reliving its memory. At times I thought their account of the events were mere forms of embellishments or hyperboles. My mind could not have conceived storm-force winds of 160 miles per hour.

A family friend who experienced the trauma of Donna Gale once told the story of a nuclear family whose roof was blown off their house in the South Hill area on that dreadful evening. In an attempt to save the life of their newborn baby, the mother wrapped the child in a blanket and handed him to her husband. Off they sped to a neighbor's house for shelter. On reaching the house, in exhaustion, the husband handed the little bundle to the neighbor. The neighbor, who was so happy that they were all alive, opened the cloth wrapping and to her dismay the baby was not in the cloth.

Along with the neighbor, the parents braved the fury of the storm and retraced their steps between their home and the neighbor's. They found the baby lying at the side of the road without a scratch.

Not all who survived Hurricane Donna were as fortunate as that child who was lost and found without injuries. There was a young man with whom I attend church who carries the psychological trauma and scare of the Donna Gale. The story was told that as a baby the noise and trauma from the hurricane affected him mentally, which adversely impacted his speech significantly. As a result, he was disallowed from receiving any formal education and had to rely on his brothers and sisters for daily sustenance.

Hurricane Donna left an enduring mark for the people of Anguilla even as they experienced the renaissance of house building. The once wooden houses with poor workmanship had to be abandoned and replaced by exterior and interior walls of six-inch cinder blocks; even the roofs that were once finished with internal polished exposed rafters and exterior galvanized sheet metal were replaced with concrete, reinforced with rebar. The design and construction of the structures, soon after the passage of Hurricane Donna, resembled caves with flat roofs. My parents, who had grown accustomed to the previous structures, found it difficult to accept the new design and preferred enjoying the romantic noise of the rain striking the galvanized sheet metal. Many complained of the heat, as most of the roofs were flat.

During the summer, one could have hardly gotten a good nap in the daytime under such roofs. Actually, in the evenings and at nights, even during the cooler months, one would go to bed in meager night clothing in preparation for the night heat from the flat concrete roof.

When I first visited Anguilla in 1970, the houses looked strange and seemed odd. They were quite big houses with flat roofs and I recall visiting a relative's house with my mom. My relative insisted we sit in the yard as she served us lemonade and snacks. Each time she exited the house she wiped her perspiration with a hand towel which remained around her neck. She finally sat to engage my mother in conversation and began wiping the perspiration that dripped from her chin to her bosom. Sighing, she uttered, "Aya, Lard, this place hot and the concrete roof mek it worse."

However, over the years few have adjusted to flat concrete roofs; the more modern concrete roofs are gable, hipped, gambrel, mansard, butterfly, shed and many more shapes and designs.

The events of Hurricane Luis, which annihilated Anguilla on September 4th to 6th, 1995, were sleeping in the recesses of the minds of those of us who had witnessed the devastation and experienced the pain of that Category Four storm. It had rested on Anguilla for approximately thirty-six hours, with most of the damage occurring after the eye of the storm passed.

I took my family to the in-laws' house to wait out that storm. The airwaves were buzzing. Social media was then a communication tool in the not-too-distant future; hence, landline telephones were our main means of audio communication. As I had never experienced a storm before, like the children of today I actually wanted the storm to visit Anguilla. When the front portion of the storm passed, I walked out of the house and was ready to get in my vehicle after taunting my father-in-law that the event was not as horrific as I thought. At that point he cautioned me not to leave his premises as yet, we had not experienced the worst. He cautioned me in a fearful voice and implored me to heed to his plea. As he was my senior, I reluctantly obeyed.

Very caringly he assisted us back into his house; I heard the barking of a hundred dogs, the hissing of many cats combined with a noise like the rolling of one hundred eighteen-wheel trucks as that terror of nature gave its last blow to our tiny island of Anguilla. From a crack in one of the living room shutters, I peeped out to observe galvanized sheet metal, plywood and various forms of debris whizzing like missiles through the air. I beckoned to my father-in-law to have a glimpse of the destruction in progress. The moment he peeped he sadly commented, "The galvanized sheet metal from the Methodist Church roof at South Hill is gone; I hope the wood on the roof is still intact." I was afraid he would have collapsed had I informed my father-in-law it was not the galvanized sheet metal from the Methodist Church but from his newly constructed apartment building.

When my father-in-law became more relaxed I told him his entire roof was gone and he needed to settle his mind on restoring it. He looked at me in disbelief and went back to our peephole and with all the anxiety in him his mind's eye showed him the roof was intact. At that point he turned and said to me, "Chris, my age may have dimmed my sight but this is one time my sight is much better than yours; my roof is intact; praise God!" Approximately half an hour later he retired to his reclining chair and, holding a towel to his forehead, asked if he could have another peep. I declined his request and told him to have his mind prepared for anything.

When the storm was over, he went to his apartment building and, after viewing the destruction, he quickly went to bed for the entire day. The following morning, as early as the sun rose, he went into the village and called his carpenter. He was determined to restore his apartment building using the same material. He reconstructed the building and after its completion he boasted of the strengthening method he had instituted.

As one drove through the island in the aftermath of Hurricane Luis, the sound of recovery could be heard all around. The pain of the storm was soon gone as the natives and residents of this island set about rebuilding the nation.

On November 18th, 1999, Hurricane Lenny, with winds of 125 miles per hour struck Anguilla. On reaching the island, it weakened and poured torrential rain on the land. Dutch St. Maarten, which is in very close proximity to Anguilla, recorded rainfall of approximately 27.56 inches. The Valley, which is Anguilla's capital, and East End were flooded. We were taught in school that Anguilla was not susceptible to flooding due to its limestone nature, but Hurricane Lenny defied that assertion. The level of water on land was so high that the fishermen took their small boats with oars and outboard motors and cruised in the water. The preparation for Hurricane Lenny was not as intense as the previous hurricanes. Nonetheless, the cost in damages to livestock, crops and houses was unexpectedly high. Actually, one of Anguilla's major five-star resorts, CuisinArt Resort and Spa (renamed CuisinArt Golf Resort and Spa), had to delay its opening due to the effects of this storm; it finally commenced operations on 20th December, 1999.

It's amazing how the human mind works. I guess it would be best explained by drawing on the comparison of a mother in labor. That mother will scream, scratch and scrabble at anyone in her path during the pain and agony of birthing a baby. But soon after the child is born, the thought of the pain is hidden in her memory. We often spoke of Hurricane Luis and educated our children, who at the time of its passage were either too small to comprehend its experience or in the "unborn world." The reinforcement of the message of pain and hurt of the storms has always been talked about, particularly by our parents, who had experienced storms of mammoth magnitude and would always find it necessary to inform us of such devastation.

CHAPTER IV

ANNOYANCE

During Hurricane Irma, we were all glued to social media, which transmitted information in real time. The transistor radios were no match for social media. As a matter of fact, the transistor radios were feeding from social media. The Facebook video postings of the storm's activity were disheartening.

The Terrorist, Hurricane Irma, was rather erratic in her motion. I recall going into work and, during our morning briefing, I informed the team that a hurricane was on the horizon which seemed pretty dangerous, and that we needed to keep an eye on it. However, we all cited it as one that followed no direct path and might not make landfall. The threat of a storm was received with little merit. However, as the general manager was unfamiliar with the weather patterns of the Caribbean, he instantly grew concerned, as did the expatriate employees.

The Anguilla Disaster Preparedness Department did provide adequate notice on radio and social media platforms; however, one can never dispense enough information when a storm of this magnitude is fast approaching its target. Further, the nationals had grown weary of hearing of storms and making the necessary preparations, but then the island would not get a drop of rain, much less wind. Hence, whilst some properties made the necessary preparations with urgency and avoided last-minute encumbrances, many of the nationals thought either the weatherman was exaggerating the virulence of the storm or the storm would pass far north of Anguilla. These assumptions were predicated on previous storms' trajectories. And it is important to be reminded that the preparation for storms can be costly and wearisome, particularly if the preparation is being made in vain.

I remember August 25th to September 8th of 1979, when voices over airwaves bellowed the co-ordinates of a potentially dangerous storm, ultimately issuing storm watches and storm warnings for the Northern Leeward Islands, which included Anguilla. It was a Category Five Hurricane named David, which was deemed to be a storm of catastrophic proportions, and all the islands in its path were cautioned of its danger and urged to take the necessary preparatory measures. I had only recently arrived on Anguilla as a sixteen-year-old lad joining my family. My dad secured all his livestock and the concrete rented house in which we lived was all boarded up, as the windows all around were of glass design. The island grew quite dark in the evening and, as my siblings and I had never experienced a hurricane, we were all excited for this experience of a lifetime. The night fell and my dad dimmed the lamp which sat on the living room center table and we were asked to go to bed. The island experienced a few gusts of wind and a bit of rain and it was soon over. It was the most annoying and upsetting occasion I can ever recall. Soon the sheets of plywood that protected the glass windows and doors were removed and life returned to normal. This monstrosity of a storm did strike some of the Caribbean islands, including the Dominican Republic, at a Category Five status and along paths of the United States of America. The sustained damages exceeded one and a half billion dollars (US) and there were more than two thousand deaths.

From September 10th to September 25th of 1989 the airwaves hyped a powerful storm coming off Cape Verde named Hurricane Hugo. Hammers were heard echoing through the various villages as Anguillians began preparing for this ferocious hurricane. Everyone was trying to protect their property and livestock. The goats that ran wild through the streets were tethered to posts that formed the structure of their sheds. Fortunately for the island, the preparations were in vain as we escaped the wrath of that Category Five hurricane. However, many of our students who were pursuing tertiary education in the United States Virgin Islands had to return home, as both St. Thomas and St. Croix were annihilated by the storm. Montserrat, a small British overseas island in the Leeward Island chain, received the full brunt of its wrath. Whilst the total death toll left in its path was a little over sixty, the damages caused exceeded ten billion dollars (US).

In September of 1998, Hurricane George was a Category Four storm which was deemed to be quite dangerous and the deadliest of the hurricane season. Its trajectory had included Anguilla. The stories told of Donna Hurricane (often referred to as Donna Gale) were enough to scare anyone to take the necessary precautionary measures. The Disaster Preparedness Department was then of little significance in terms of its organization; hence, the tales of past storms and their coordinates took precedence as to how the nationals viewed the danger of any impending storms. When Hurricane George struck Antigua, there was much alarm among the population. However, when the storm began pounding on St. Kitts and Nevis, information was swiftly made available to Anguilla by families and friends resident in these islands by way of telephone until the storm soon took its toll on this utility. Again, hammers were heard in every village and trucks began lining up at the hardware stores in search of nails and ply-wood. These stores quickly ran out of supplies as they were ill prepared for such last-minute emergency demands. As a result, some houses or buildings were only casually prepared if the storm would have struck the island. Albert Lake's petrol-filling station in The Valley was lined with vehicles in wait to have their fuel tanks filled. Many waited as long as two to three hours to be served with petrol. On learning of the death toll of over six hundred persons and the damages left in its path, totaling a little under ten billion dollars (US), we thought ourselves fortunate. It did pain us for the lives and damages it inflected on our neighboring islands, and we undoubtedly provided financial and other assistance in our small way.

The constant preparation for hurricanes has always been a costly exercise on islands that have populations with minuscule earnings. As one person stated, when Anguillians said "Aya Lard" in those days it signaled there was no way of escaping such dangers.

CHAPTER V

THE DAY OF RECKONING

Radio Anguilla was on the alert to provide the necessary status of the Terrorist Irma, and so was social media, including Facebook, Twitter and Google. The National Oceanographic and Atmospheric Administration was the main feature on the television screens in almost every home and place of business. The politics of America, its House and Senate discussions or hearings on the Russians assisting Donald Trump to win the 2016 presidential elections had now become of little significance.

Anguilla, celebrating its Golden Jubilee signifying its secession from the twin-island state of St. Kitts and Nevis, portrayed a sense of pride. The revolution of 1967 was a feature that took center stage from the beginning of 2017. Sadly, the Father of the Nation, Mr. James Ronald Webster, who played a pivotal role in the revolution, was buried at the beginning of the year. Whilst 2017 was meant to be a year of reflection on the progress the island had made over the period, some of the citizens thought the island had regressed and took their grievances to the airwaves. The talk shows, including "To The Point," "On The Spot," "The Mayor Show" and the "DJ Hammer Midmorning Show," were used as platforms for the nationals to air their thoughts on the regression of the revolution.

It was sensed that the reason behind the outburst was due to the politics of the day. The Anguilla Day Celebration on May 30th, 2017 was met with distractions. A small group of concerned Anguillians conducted a quiet and orderly march in demonstration of their view that the direction Anguilla had taken under Chief Minister Victor Banks' administration had been against the tenets of the revolution. Conversely, the stadium of James Ronald Webster's Park was packed to capacity by celebrants who thought the island had progressed significantly and as a people all should unite around a common purpose. The trumpeted phrase was likened to the writing on a United States of America coin: "E pluribus unum" (out of many, one). Whilst ideas differed, it was necessary to move forward with one voice and a single determination in the promotion of a better nation socially, politically and economically.

Economically, the island was facing severe hardship. The government of the day had made promises: a higher standard of living; ridding the masses of undue tax burdens, including a tax called "The Stabilization Levy," which had been instituted by its predecessor; a more modern labor code would be implemented after decades of delay; and a marketing strategy to revitalize the struggling tourism industry would be enacted as well as a resolution to the banking crisis. The impatience of the people coupled with political agendas created a sour counterpoint to the celebration.

During the celebration, the leader of the opposition made it a point of duty to represent the cause of those who wished to be on the other side of history; in a failed attempt she sought to recognize the protestors and was met with taunting by the masses. She tried to get her point across but was stifled by the loud jeering of the crowd. She soon took her seat and waited for the Chief Minister to rebuke the crowd for their outburst. To her dismay and to that of her meager group of supporters, he passed on this opportunity and allowed democracy to prevail; citizens were free to demonstrate on either side and "let the chips fall where they may."

Furthermore, at a special service held in honor of the Jubilee Celebration, Chief Minister Banks, in response to those who were in defiance of the celebration, expressed his counter-defiance with the colloquial expression, "If they don't like it, let them lump it." The latter was like waving a red flag at a raging bull. This expression lit up the airwaves and the talk shows took him to task for such remarks that they claimed hurt to the core. I often thought had there not been a celebration the government would have been forced to demit office "en mass." It was clear that the masses wished to be on the "right side of history."

One of the things that continues to confuse our youth is the history of the revolution. As it is often mentioned, "Until lions can talk, history will always be written by the hunters." This cliché holds true with Anguilla's revolution; however, the nation celebrates nonetheless.

The fear of the impending Terrorist, Hurricane Irma, brought about the suspension of all the negative talks and actions surrounding the celebration. The real religious feelings of the Anguillian public became alive as the radio stations very quickly played religious songs. On every street corner and in almost every place of business the buzz words were echoed in question form: "Are you ready for the storm?" I recall casually walking up to the cashier at one of the island's prominent places of business and hearing her informing a customer of the aisle where flashlights were shelved. With a chuckling disdain, she replied, "Who de hell you tellin' 'bout flashlight; say dat to the weak hearts; no damn storm a come ya. A year me live a Anguilla and hear 'bout storm a-come and none come. Me wouldn't bar up a friggin 'ting." I grew scared for her.

Having returned to the island on the eve of Irma from a New York trip where my mother was honored as an outstanding educator, I embraced my wife and would soon to be greeted by my daughter, whom I refer to as a "fearless attorney," and my last emboldened seventeen-year-old son. They backed down from no discussion but failed to mention the impending Terrorist. The evening of the 5th of September, a video surfaced on Facebook and other social media platforms displaying sadly the pummeling of Barbuda, the sister island of Antigua. In disbelief, I made calls to a few of my colleagues who thought the clipping was from an old Chinese movie and that its posting on such sites was intended to scare residents who were in the path of this deadly storm. The clipping showed trees being blown about, forty-foot containers winging through the air along with cars, concrete structures collapsing and persons screaming and alerting others of the impending danger. I guess the voices were not audible or were garbled by wind;

hence, many thought it was indeed a hoax. Only later in the evening did we learn it was factual.

Hammers and saws were heard throughout the island. Contractors who sat idle for years became active, as their skills were now required to secure homes and businesses. Plywood was in great demand as many of the homes used massive windows in order for residents to enjoy the sunlight peering through in the morning and at noonday. Very important for the locals are the beautiful sunsets of this little island and the natives enjoy sharing them with tourists. Living in Anguilla's west, it is easy to look through one's window and observe the final descent of the sun below the horizon. The natives joke about the flash of the setting sun as they claim, "With the beauty of Anguilla and its people, God takes a picture of it every time the sun hits the horizon to boast of his creation to the rest of the world."

My wife called on her workmen to get the family home secured as I contended with the preparatory work at my workplace, Zemi Beach House Hotel on Shoal Bay. I must admit, when I arrived home she had left nothing for me to do. I applauded her for all her efforts but to some extent felt I had failed as her partner in carrying out my duty to ensure the safety of my family. She soon told me not to worry. She understood that my task as the second-in-command at my place of work was demanding and needed my attention.

It was amazing, the manner in which some of the guests responded to the call to evacuate the island. A couple at one of the properties was ambivalent to the evacuation call. They were having a great time indeed. He was an aged gentleman of about seventy-five enjoying a rendezvous with a twenty-five-year-old lady. In his passion he openly stated, "I want to ride through the storm." The young lady, running her hand through his implanted hair and groping him as she sat on his knees at the bar, said romantically, "Baby I yearn for us to be a storm in that storm." His eyes twinkled at the thought of her sentiments. I feared for them both. It was evident, no matter the wealth one possesses, that storms of Hurricane Irma's nature came only to kill, steal and destroy everything in their path. I grew more concerned as they began to romance each other; the passions grew hotter as they both decided to continue the process in the confines of their suite. I was left dumbfounded as I churned over in my mind the destruction that could befall these two even during moments of passion. I beckoned to him to be careful as he retorted, "Chris, it will be a great way to die, in a storm of this nature, in my baby's arms."

They both eventually left the resort and the island unhappily under the threat of the innkeeper's use of security assistance.

The Day of Reckoning

CHAPTER VI

NAIL-BITING EXPERIENCE

In the early afternoon of September 5, 2017, I hunkered down with the family, expecting the worse and never letting on. Around 5 p.m. the skies grew dark as the storm clouds gathered. I called to my son, Kohn, and asked for his description of the clouds. He looked toward the skies and stated, "Dad, there is a storm coming, don't ask me anything about clouds, this is not any time for a classroom session."

I saw the deep concern on my son's face and thought I would provide some distraction, but it didn't work. He was focused on the potential intensity of the storm. I remained jovial whilst my son became upset. I told him there was no need to get upset as he believed in euthanasia and he is a strong supporter of a true liberal society. I attempted to tease him and told him the worst that can happen in the storm is death. His response was venomous. He said, "You hate the idea of anyone using cannabis whilst I have often purported failure to allow someone to choose their destiny is an infringement on his or her rights." He argued with passion, citing the various uses of this illegal substance. He ended his discussion by calling it a tranquilizer. I had an anxiety check at that moment and timidly asked him if he had ever used that substance; he vehemently responded, "Dad, I have never tried it and will never do so, but I will respect all men, those who use and those who don't."

As I was now convinced he would not use such a substance, I told him many might be using it during the storm. He retorted, "Dad, any man taking a 'blunt' during this time will only be wasting his money. The magnitude of this storm will not allow any tranquilizer to function at this time; the storm wants everyone to be conscious of its arrival and so it will be."

My wife asked if any would like to have cereal with warm milk before she had the cooking gas disconnected. Kohn declined the offer and, at that point, I realized the impending storm was affecting his ability to function normally. He does not refuse food at all and cornflakes with warm milk at that time of the evening was his favorite snack. As we had all moved downstairs on the ground floor of the house, I asked that he go upstairs and retrieve the keyboard, guitar and my saxophone. At that point he indicated to me that my mobile phone was ringing. It was a former guest from one of the previous resorts where I had worked. He is a prolific writer and whilst I do not mix work with friendship we became friends due to the many commonalities among us.

Karp is quite jovial and is an extrovert. In his husky voice, he said with a chuckle, "Enjoy Hurricane Irma and write everything. Have fun!" Later I received a text from him stating, "Praying for you!" Karp had never seemed to be the religious type, so I thought his statement was nothing but a cliché. However, he alerted me to turn the negatives of the storm into a learning experience and share it across the globe. The safety of me and my family demanded my attention. But, on second thought I decided to record the good, the bad and the ugly events of Terrorist Hurricane Irma.

I soon reclined on the bed with the entire family. We enjoy singing at times; hence, Kohn grabbed his guitar. In harmony, we all began singing that familiar song of Bob Marley, "Don't worry about a thing 'cause every little thing gonna be alright." I pulled my saxophone to my lips and at intervals blew in a jovial manner. The lights in the room began to flicker and soon there was no electricity. I playfully shouted, "Electricity, where are you? Please get back here!" Kohn looked at me in disgust as he shot back, "Dad, this is serious, it is not a joking matter; put that saxophone down." The kids thought I was too funny for the occasion so they soon left me blowing the saxophone alone. My wife looked at me in disbelief and asked that I get serious. Actually, I was trying to ease the tension in the room that was growing at an astronomical rate. I soon thought I would need another tactic to bring some calm to the family.

As my wife moved around in the room which we called our bunker, I remembered the clock striking at 2:00 a.m. I curled myself in the bed in my underwear and was all happy to nod away to sleep. The dreams were sweet. It is said that the longest dreams last for only twenty-two seconds but I believed I dreamt for hours unending. I am not usually a light sleeper regardless of the surroundings. Once sleep enters my eyes I am "dead to the world." However, the danger of this Terrorist caused me to be alert even in my sleep. Foggily, I could hear things being thrown around outside by the storm.

Around 4:00 a.m. my wife pulled me by my feet and alerted me to be prepared as it was her view that we best vacate the bedroom. I was highly upset with her as she was actually disturbing me from the safe haven of dreamland. However, I decided to yield to her commands and the demands of the Terrorist, Hurricane Irma.

As I arose to my feet the secured window over the bed was attacked. The storm began pulling on the plywood that protected the window.

Within seconds, we left all our belongings in the eastern bedroom and headed to the western one. While we were escaping our dash was slowed by the suction of the wind. Suddenly, I heard the sound of glass shattering behind us. My daughter DeLeon exclaimed while we were on the move, "Dad, get your computer and saxophone!" I hastily responded, "Those are replaceable items, DeLe! Run!"

On arriving in the other bedroom I reached for my telephone which carried a Digicel chip and noticed I had lost the signal. I turned to my wife and asked if she had telephone signal on her mobile. She doubted but checked and noted that her mobile with a chip from the company FLOW had a strong signal. I quickly got her mobile and called my place of work and was not able to reach anyone. The Digicel signal was gone throughout the island. I called my sister, Grace, who lived in the South Hill area. She informed me her bedroom windows and door had been sucked out of the house along with pieces of clothing. She and her husband had obviously abandoned their nine-hundred-square-feet bedroom and lodged themselves under an interior stairwell having twenty-five square feet of standing space.

I felt rather helpless as I considered the destruction the island was receiving at the hands of Terrorist Irma. I called my parents and received a response from Iva, my sister, whose house is separated from my parents' by a flower garden. She informed me that they were secured in her house, which had a concrete roof.

I began to imagine my dad's state of mind. He believed strongly in connecting with the earth through gardening. Hence, he had banana, plantain and avocado trees growing in his garden. I inquired of my sister on the condition of his produce garden and she quickly avoided my questions. It was clear from the tone of her voice she wished for strength to continue to face this all-out war Terrorist Irma had unleashed on this tiny island of ours.

Meanwhile at my house, one of the ladies desired to use the bathroom. I asked if they could hold on for a few moments as the bathroom was about to be attacked. As we sheltered in the western bedroom we listened to the madness that was taking place in the previous room. We began to forecast the destruction, as the internet had now been interrupted and Radio Anguilla had long left the airwaves in our area of Rendezvous West. Radio Lazer 101 on St. Martin was now silent as well; the commentators who kept us company and provided the tracking information during the front end of the storm had their reach yanked from them. There was a sense of isolation from the happenings and this obviously contributed significantly to the increased anxiety in the room.

My son, Kohn, grabbed the battery-operated radio and began moving its dial frantically in an effort to find a radio station that had not succumbed to the attacks of Terrorist Hurricane Irma. In his bewilderment he cast the radio aside and stated, "Guys, all media reach is lost, we now have to be guided by our own intuition." He sternly pointed to me and stated firmly, "Dad, no joke! The storm is getting hotter!" I exclaimed, "Nothing can get hotter than this; I do believe we have passed the worst."

The winds had somewhat subsided slightly. I asked that all take a bathroom break and my wife interjected, "Only if you have to do so. The worst is ahead of us." I grew upset at her, as it was my view that she was about to reignite fear in the room. I looked at her with a stern eye and before I managed to get out one word she quickly reminded me of Hurricane Luis of 1995. She normally has great intuition on matters of this nature. She was raised in an extended family structure with a father who was very senior and a grandmother who enjoyed a life spanning some ninety years. Hence, she brought realities to our fears as she recounted stories of the elderly who had observed storms and their patterns. She made it clear that it was possible that the storm had shifted and part of the eye might be imminent. All were guided by her judgement and decided to remain in the room.

Nail-Biting Experience

CHAPTER VII

THE MIDST OF THE STORM

We had nervously wandered out into the living room; I thought it was a good time for a little humor and I began to tease all regarding the prospects that the storm would have devastated the island. I felt like there was some destruction but thought it was minimal. I soon heard doors banging and debris flying.

I ran back to my sanctuary in the room, followed by my kids. My wife and her mom remained, as they were recovering from the shock of it all. The fury with which the winds blew and howled demanded everyone's attention except my mother-in-law's, who at this time was completely exhausted. The sound of the wind was scary; it sounded like a thousand and one demons traveling together. My mind quickly took me back to a movie I had seen as a preteen, "Twilight Zone." Having seen it once, I promised never to look at it again; it cost me many sleepless nights. I had to get a hold of myself and realize I was forty-plus years out of my teens and had to face this Terrorist like a man. However, the question came to me so pointedly: "How does one not respond to nature's fury?"

All four of us recognized our energies were being sapped and we needed a lever that would assist us in conserving what was left of our strength. As three held the door closed, my wife, despite her fright, mustered the energy to push a weighted chest of drawers against the heavy wooden door. And we all sat on it to provide more resistance against those demons. All began praying, some openly and others quietly.

The fight against nature's terror cannot be met with physical force and that made me angry. I am a fighter and I am always on guard for any challenge life presents. However, I was trapped in my own conceit and anguish, knowing fully well I couldn't fight back. I began covertly cursing the Terrorist. Soon I recalled the passage of scripture where the Bible character Job was experiencing some serious storms in his life, and when he couldn't physically fight back, he questioned nature's anger towards him. The God he served for many years spoke to him even in his pain, as noted in Job 38:

Then the Lord spoke to Job out of the storm. He said,

"Who is this that obscures with words without knowledge?

Brace yourself like a man; I will question you, and you shall answer me.

Where were you when I laid the earth's foundation? Tell me if you understand.

Who marked off its dimensions? Surely you know! Who stretched a measuring line across it?

On what were its footings set, or who laid its cornerstone while the morning stars sang together and all the angels shouted for joy?

Who shut up the sea behind doors when it burst forth from the womb..."

It was consoling but I couldn't get the courage to share it with my family for fear it would only engender more anxiety. I recognized I was the leader in this effort to calm all fears and I was running out of ways and means of placating the overwhelming anxiety. I was deeply encouraged by my son, who observed my resilience was being heavily challenged and decided to take the lead in fighting against the force of nature by placing his muscular body at the forefront of the battle in ensuring our security was not hindered in the room. It was a sight to see muscles being replaced by fat. The energies from my fat were soon depleted.

Whilst applying the necessary energies to the door I heard my wife crying out in the dimly lighted room, "Chris, my ears are hurting badly and they're getting clogged; please, my ear drums are pounding." At this point I was at my wit's end. I know my wife would only cry out on last resort; hence, I sought a consensus over opening one of the windows slightly. Within two minutes it was discussed, including the possible ramifications, and I made the final call to open the window.

On opening the window, my wife did give a sigh of relief and thanked me for yielding to her request. However, while I was happy to be able to source a panacea for her earache, I began to give second thoughts to my actions as she began asking questions randomly that in my view had no bearing on the crucial matter at hand. Soon my son released himself of holding the door and had an outburst. The actions of this Terrorist were really hitting him where it hurts.

He threw himself on the bed with his grandmother and angrily exclaimed, "I am tired and want this thing to stop. Can someone tell me when this will all be over? I never want to go through anything like this again." I was dumbfounded and accepted his question as rhetorical. I thought the best thing I could do was to remain quiet, as I recalled the saying that had been so often used by my deceased grandmother, "Silence does not signify weakness, most times it contributes to peace." I wished there were lines of communication to the outside of the room but there were none, which caused our frustration to escalate. Soon my daughter commented, "The radio did say it wouldn't last long." We remained quiet at this time as the horror of nature's act seemed to have exceeded a couple of days.

However, my courage was bolstered even though the energies I was drawing from my son had failed. As a church boy, the scripture began to haunt me about King David when the Amalekites had attacked Ziklag and destroyed it; as a result, King David's own people lost the energies necessary to fight and he had to find courage in his God (1 Samuel 30:6). Deep within I pleaded to God for courage to battle the storm, and my petition was granted.

Through a peephole in the door, I saw the wind accompanied by water ferociously blowing into my living room from the window in the eastern bedroom, unhinging my front door as it swept away everything in its path. My wife kept asking me about the damages I was observing and I refused to respond. She had wished for me to allow her to use the peephole but I acted as if I was transfixed and could not move. Soon I felt the concrete walls of the house shaking; I was quickly reminded of the guest who lost his family in the World Trade Center in the 9/11 attack and faced the reality that it would be hard to carry on in life without my family. However, my faith or courage was not shaken, as I determined I would fight to the end.

My son began screaming from the bed to the Terrorist, "Stop! Stop! We have had enough." His exclamation meant the world to me as I noted he had been silent for almost an hour as he retreated to battle the storm in his mind. I was happy he was venting his frustration through talking to the situation at hand. I did not care if the attacking storm had no ears to hear his declaration; open venting speaks volumes in situations like these. Afterwards, he arose from the bed and repositioned himself at the door as he signaled to me to take a rest but I declined hastily. I felt I had provided a bastion of hope with regards to the family's security and to release the lead could have led to pandemonium.

The winds abated to little gusts and the silence in the room became increasingly deafening. About twenty minutes later I removed myself from the door, and my family assisted me in removing the chest of drawers which, as a combating weapon, would forever remain etched in our memories. We emerged from the room without a scratch as we tiptoed through the rubble and the broken glass that was scattered all over the living and dining rooms. I sought to access the outdoors and saw a surrounding that I just couldn't identify.

I turned to my family and scathingly stated, "Welcome to the new Anguilla; we sure have a lot of work to do."

CHAPTER VIII

THE UNVEILED DESTRUCTION

few hours had elapsed and I decided to jump into my jeep and drive around the village. The trees were leafless and the nakedness of the village was heart-wrenching. My neighbors' houses, which once seemed so far away, now appeared to be in arm's reach, as the shrubbery that bounded our properties had surrendered to the storm. I feared the worst but prayed that all lives were spared.

My son, who sat next to me, was turning the dial on the radio frantically but static dominated every setting where there had previously been a radio station. As we drove on the main road, the streets were desolate. Electrical poles lay broken across the street or lined the streets along with tree branches and roofing debris. I tried to hold on to my composure as I did not want my son to see the weak side of me; tears began to crawl over the back of my eyes and I had to tilt my head forward whilst giving a stare at the disaster. I noted the collapse of concrete walls and roofs and saw vehicles that were upturned. I was careful to note a car with its rear sitting on a wall as its front end dangled in the gently blowing wind. As I approached the upper portion of South Hill it was easy to observe forty-foot containers displaced. My little island of Anguilla resembled a war zone. It reminded me of the scenes of terrorist acts displayed on television.

In despair, I created a path to my sister's house with my jeep and inquired of her safety. It was obvious she and her husband were fine but my brother-in-law was in disbelief as he was told of his forty-foot container that was seen flying through the air like a wingless airplane. It was obvious from the final resting place of the metal container that it had to be airborne during its passage from where it had been originally.

Eventually, an increased number of cars began creating their own paths in their quest to view the devastation for one reason or another. Some did so in an effort to ensure their families and friends in other villages were safe, and others as a means of devising more devastation through looting.

Driving through the island and seeing no police officer in sight was scary. Anarchy took center stage as looting began. The bewildered faces of the drivers I crossed almost discouraged me from continuing the tour of terror. I kept eavesdropping on conversations that issued from passengers in open trucks as we crossed each other's paths at a snail's pace along the winding makeshift pathways. An elderly gentleman, his hand on his head and with tears in his eyes, bellowed, "Anguilla is no more; Lord, wha' we gonna do?"

The traffic in our area was directed by a mentally deranged man and he did a job that matched that of any law enforcement officer. Actually, I thought he was a police officer in plain clothes until my son remarked, "Dad, the storm had medicinal effects, it restored Frankie's sanity." I retorted,

"Where is he? I am sure his family got him sedated during this time." I then realized he was the man who was diverting the traffic around a pole that had blocked the main road. He walked to my car and called me by name and said, "Chris, there is a Digicel metal pole across the road and I am diverting the traffic on private property." I did not know how to respond as the last time I heard his voice was more than twenty years ago. He would usually walk the street day and night with a cigarette in the corner of his mouth as he drooled on himself.

As I drove away from him I heard drivers commenting that the hurricane may have brought destruction but it brought sanity to some. When I arrived at my parents' residence I told them of the person who made himself the traffic police and they could not believe me. My dad asked hastily, "Where were the police?" I informed him that my journey to his house may have taken two and a half hours and I had not seen a police officer or a police vehicle in sight. At the same time there was a gentleman who drove from the eastern end of the island as I drove from the west and he had confirmed that he had not seen any police vehicle along the way.

I turned to my son and said in disgust, "Kohn, this is disappointing, the police need to be on the streets." He retorted calmly, "Dad, under the uniform is a person; the terror of the storm could have sent them in a hole, they are human beings." I angrily responded, "Kohn, you are upsetting me with your response. They have sworn under oath to maintain law and order on the island of Anguilla." Kohn, pausing as he pronounced each word, calmly stated, "Dad, the officers' oath to protect and maintain the laws of Anguilla was made during peace time; had it been done whilst Hurricane Irma was hitting this country, we would not have had even a Commissioner of Police taking the oath." I pondered on Kohn's statement and preferred to drop that line of discussion; I was almost in agreement with him.

Later in the afternoon, the streets became more crowded as the sightseers increased astronomically; many of the vehicles that were being driven had no registration numbers, some had broken windscreens and heavy dents. I signaled to my son that I was uncomfortable with vehicles moving around without registration numbers and he quickly remarked that criminal activity could escalate.

Angrily, I reached into my pocket for my mobile phone and noted the telecommunication company, FLOW, was active; I dialed the police station and was disheartened that there was no answer. My son took the phone from me and noted I was dialing the wrong number. However, I thought it was foolhardy of me to entertain the thought that after such a storm the telephone poles would be standing. I had a few telephone numbers for some police friends of mine but they had Digicel telecommunication service. This provider failed early in the storm and their customers became quite upset, as their slogan read, "Bigger and Better Network." Fortunately for me I had mobile phones from multiple carriers, as I thought either or both telephone companies could have lost signals during this monstrous storm. Nonetheless, Digicel was criticized by its customers as being inefficient and its tagline was mocked as droves of their customers soon herded into the parking lot of the carrier FLOW. The slogan of FLOW seemed simple as I recall it to memory, "This is how we flow." A few of the Digicel customers requested to borrow my workable mobile phone but I was fearful that it would have gotten lost in the crowd as it was my only means of communication across the country and outside of the country.

My phone soon rang and the ring seemed aggravating. I was reluctant to answer the call but did on the fifth or sixth ring. It was a friend on the line informing me that the Terrorist Hurricane Irma had taken a life in the Stoney Ground area. It was claimed that his house collapsed on him and he succumbed to his injuries.

Quickly, I recalled a few years ago when Anguilla had had its first female Commissioner of Police ridiculed for a statement she made in an interview recorded in the *Belfast Telegraph* titled, "Ardoyne to Paradise: PSNI's Amanda takes over as top cop on Caribbean island of Anguilla..." She said, "…Anguilla is only 16 miles long by three miles wide with a population of 14,000. So everybody knows everybody. It's a village trying to be a country." Actually, this statement may have caused her to demit office prematurely and flee the country under a cloud. However, her statement was confirmed in terms of the fact that this single tragic death caused the entire island to go into mourning. At every turn, the islanders, in grief, spoke of the death of this sanitation worker, Washington, who had perished in the storm.

There were all kinds of stories surrounding his death. Being alone in his little house may have been the most contributing factor to his death. He was remembered for his candid spirit as he attended to removing the garbage from the bins in the wee hours of the morning and into the midmornings. He was fearless, strong and brave, and as a nation, while no flags were flown at half-mast, we mourned his death deeply.

In the ensuing days right after the storm, as I continued to transverse the island, I observed most of the government buildings, including schools, seaports and the main police station. However, I decided to park outside the disheveled Blowing Point terminal building where a few taxi drivers stood in bewilderment. It is estimated that more than eighty percent of our tourists use this port. We all stood there and the silence was deafening. Soon one of the taxi drivers opined, "There goes our tourist season for 2017 to 2018, Chris." He paused for my response as I retorted, "Let's keep the faith and hope for the best." One of the drivers in despair stated, "Anguilla done; she finish." An argument erupted as most of the taxi drivers sought to instill hope into the young man's mind. He soon walked away, unconvinced that Anguilla would arise from its ashes very quickly.

I slumped over my car's steering wheel as a young man came over and told the story of a mother's deep and unwavering love for her child. He claimed that during the storm a little boy requested of his mother the use of the bathroom. A few minutes later she heard a crashing sound and ran to her son's rescue. The child was trapped in the bathroom by galvanized metal sheets and broken pieces of wood which resulted from the collapsed living room ceiling of the house. The mother braved the horror of the storm and pushed away the debris in an effort to rescue her son. After she retrieved him from the bathroom, on her way back to the bedroom she observed their only bastion was a closet. She placed her son in the closet and was struck by a piece of wood with protruding galvanized nails which dug into her back; she was resolute in providing the necessary safety for her son even if it meant sacrificing her life.

When the storm subsided she observed she was standing in a pool of blood and was convinced it was not hers, but it was, to her dismay. She was soon weakened due to the loss of blood and managed to reach the hospital for treatment. On arriving there she noticed portions of the hospital room had been destroyed by the Terrorist Hurricane Irma. She recovered with the joy that her son was left unharmed.

One of the taxi drivers, on hearing the story, said, "Just like how that lady did everything to save her son, we will do everything to resurrect this island; we will not lose hope. We are ready to rebuild." That sparked extra courage in me that all was not lost. In Anguilla we often say, "When the taxi drivers speak, you better listen."

One of the island's top radio stations was now on the airwaves and began detailing the damages. There was much static on the line but I thought I misunderstood the radio announcer when he stated that most or all of the churches on the island had been damaged. However, he repeated the statement and I sought to confirm his assertion via social media. At that point I remembered my dad's phrase that he would use every so often, "Whenever there is no information, misinformation prevails." Facebook and other social media platforms were at least as credible as the mainstream media. Hence, I drove from the west end portion of the island to the eastern portion and observed many of the churches were indeed damaged. Among some of the places of worship with notable damages included the Long Bay Seventh Day Adventist Church, The Road Methodist Church and The Valley Methodist Church, which had been recorded as one of the oldest churches on the island.

The damage to the churches fueled some of the talk show hosts for the ensuing days. One of the hosts, who was quite religious, claimed the storm was God's judgement on Anguilla. He was obviously called out for such an unfounded and frivolous assertion. Some members of the religious community used their pulpits on the following Sunday morning to respond to such idle propaganda. I thought it strange that he could have made such an assertion. It was later purported that he received injuries during the storm that affected his ability to walk normally. Nonetheless, some stood in defense of his statement that the storm was God's punishment on the island of Anguilla, to the dismay of many in the Christian Community.

However, the talk was soon diluted into oblivion as most of the pastors across the island assured their parishioners that what the island may have experienced was similar to that of Job in the Bible. I sat in a church meeting and heard a preacher informing his parishioners that it was needless for them to view the storm as God's judgement on the nation and he called for his congregation to avoid self-pity and self-condemnation as he referenced the story of Job in the Holy Scriptures.

The despair on every street corner, in every village and hamlet, was palpable. Yet behind the fears, all were cautioned to lift up their heads and begin to rebuild and to listen to the words of solace from the clergy, the politicians, friends and visitors of Anguilla. I was further moved by the many calls I received from former tourists who were deeply concerned about our well-being. Many wished to make donations and were willing to offer all the assistance they could. Some of the most memorable calls were from Suzan, Charlie and Aileen. They expressed deep concerns about the livelihood of the nationals of the island and hoped that the hospitality business would rebound soonest.

The Unveiled Destruction

CHAPTER IX

THE BRITISH ON THE GROUND

The roaring of the helicopter overhead was a vivid reminder to the Anguillian baby boomers of the events of the revolution of 1967 when the British troops landed on the island. But in 2017, while their presence was welcomed, many of the nationals thought the mother country, the United Kingdom, was sluggish in its response to the catastrophe the island had recently faced.

The chopper overhead was privy to an aerial view of the disaster and flew as close as possible to the ground. In the distance on the sea was a British frigate. I parked my jeep on the side of the road, as the tears in my eyes had blurred my vision for a moment. Fortunately for the island, most people had built up supplies of canned food and water as mandated by the Hurricane Preparedness Committee which was managed under the Governor's office.

A very salient point to be made was the abundance of care that was exhibited among the natives for each other. It was palpable. Many began sharing what they had stored, not knowing how the stock would be replenished.

The talk shows soon started their rhetoric regarding the British treatment of Anguilla. They declared that the British had adopted the "stepchild" attitude. Soon, one of the British aircraft landed with the British foreign secretary, Mr. Boris Johnson. He was given a dignitary's welcome as he was met on the tarmac by the chief minister, the Honorable Victor Banks. Rumor soon spread across the island that the chief minister had informed the British government that Anguilla was not in need of its assistance. The chief minister's effort to stifle this rumor was met with skepticism. However, it was apparently propagated because the chief minister came to the defense of the British in informing the nationals that he thought they responded to the disaster in a timely manner. Mr. Banks, in a press conference, stated that the storm ended around 3:00 p.m. on Wednesday September 6th, 2017, and that by 5:00 p.m. of that same day Secretary Johnson had called him and assured him of the British intention to stand by Anguilla during the difficult times. Mr. Banks was adamant that the island was in need of financial and technical assistance in order for the lives of the residents to return to normalcy in record time. Actually, the chief minister vehemently rejected the British proposal of providing £32 million sterling pounds to be shared among all the overseas countries that were distressed by the passage of Hurricane Irma. This was made known to the media which was noted in *The Guardian* [1].

The chief minister did present his argument for increased aid in an open letter which was shared in *The Anguillian*, the island's local newspaper. It is important to note that, in terms of government receipts and expenditure, it was on a good track. Its approved budget for 2017 showed revenue collections at EC$214.90m with a recurrent expenditure of EC$211.96m. In pleading with the British Government, Chief Minister Banks stated in his letter:

> The June revised forecast projected recurrent revenue to be EC$206.72m, recurrent expenditure at EC$198.88m and a revised budget surplus of EC$7.84m. At the end of August mere days before Hurricane Irma the recurrent accounts were in a position of EC$18.17m surplus, significantly above the period estimate of EC$5.42m. Overall, the damage and losses in Anguilla are so severe that it will require financial assistance from the United Kingdom Government (UKG) in the short to medium term if we are to protect jobs, livelihoods and incomes and prevent a full-scale economic and social crisis. Indeed, our mindset is to turn this negative into a positive by securing for Anguilla the economic and social infrastructure required for sustainable development. We therefore table the following for 2008.

> In light of the anticipated budget shortfalls, the Government of Anguilla is requesting that the United Kingdom Government provides a recurrent budget support line to Anguilla as the need arises over the next 12 to 18 months.

Renovation and Reconstruction of Homes: United Kingdom Government to provide grant funds to enable the Government of Anguilla to in turn provide grants to persons who are not financially able to renovate and reconstruct their homes. United Kingdom Government to also provide grant funds to enable Government of Anguilla to provide a capital injection to the Anguilla Development Board (ADB), which in turn loans funds at concessionary rates to enable persons to renovate and reconstruct their homes.

The six Government Primary Schools and the Secondary School were damaged and in some cases will have to be completely rebuilt. This is a high priority area, as the aim is to have the rebuilt schools ready for the start of the 2018/2019 academic year. The Government Hospital was also damaged and this served to highlight that this facility has served its useful life and needs to be replaced by a modern one fit for purpose facility.

Small Business Support: UKG assistance is requested to provide a grant to GoA to provide capital injection to ADB to provide loans to small businesses to repair and reconstruct their facilities and to replace inventory lost.

The Anguilla Electricity Company, which is majority owned by Government of Anguilla, suffered extensive damage to its transmission and distribution network. In fact, it is estimated that it will take up to six months to fully restore electricity throughout the island. With hurricanes such as Irma expected to become the norm rather than exception it is prudent that if Anguilla is to rebuild stronger and more resiliently, then an assessment should be made of the costs of putting electricity in key areas underground. Government of Anguilla is therefore requesting United Kingdom Government grant assistance to conduct the assessment and to help fund the required investment.

Sea Ports Development – In 2016 the UKG pledged to provide capital grant assistance to GoA to construct a new cargo pier at Road Bay. Due to the passage of Irma and other reasons progress with this project has been delayed. Government of Anguilla is requesting that these funds be carried over so that Anguilla can benefit from this project which is crucial to ensuring that Anguilla's only port of entry for goods is up to the requisite standard and requirements. Blowing Point Port, which is the main gateway for Anguillians and tourists to the island, suffered the loss of the terminal facility which again had outlived its useful life. The Caribbean Development Bank Board had approved the Blowing Point

Port Ferry Terminal Loan in 2008 but the United Kingdom Government disallowed due to the impact of the 2008 global financial and economic crisis.

Prior to the passage of Hurricane Irma I had made the extension of the runway (along with support terminal and other facilities) at the Clayton Lloyd Airport a priority with the view of enabling Anguilla to have a more robust tourism economy. This question of adequate air access to Anguilla has been thrown into sharp relief as Anguilla's primary hub, Princess Juliana International Airport in neighboring Dutch St. Maarten, has been closed since the passage of Hurricane Irma and is expected to remain closed for some time. Government of Anguilla is therefore requesting the United Kingdom Government grant assistance to extend the runway at Clayton Lloyd Airport to a length that will support and enhance Anguilla's immediate national security needs, enhance Anguilla's growth prospects and reduce Anguilla's over reliance on its neighbours for economic security. Also, as an intervention in the immediate term the Government of Anguilla would be grateful if the United Kingdom Government can give consideration to financing the 2017 costs of the ongoing Air Traffic Control and Fire Hall project at the Airport (United Kingdom

Government funded the costs of this project up to 2016 and Government of Anguilla had requested continued assistance in 2017 but this was declined).

Mr. Banks letter continued: Since 2008 Government of Anguillan has had in place a Master Plan for the Valley Roads Project which was the subject of an United Kingdom Foreign and Commonwealth Office funded 'value for money assessment' in 2012. However, this project has been continually deferred because of lack of financial resources. Proceeding now would allow the Valley Town to have this crucial infrastructure with the added benefit of putting in the requirements for underground electric cable.

Reconstruction of Government Office Accommodation – A number of Government buildings including the Governor's Office Complex (which seats Executive Council Chambers), the Police Headquarters and the complex housing the Anguilla House of Assembly and Courts have been damaged extensively. This provides the opportunity for Government to do a comprehensive Master Plan and development of modern office accommodation to optimize productivity and reduce costs; currently Government rents a number of private facilities which adds to its recurrent costs.

Replacement of the Vehicle Fleet – GoA's Vehicle Fleet, already woefully inadequate and outdated, suffered extensive damage as a result of Hurricane Irma.

Lord Ahmad, the areas mentioned are not an exhaustive list of what is required to put Anguilla on the path to sustainable development. And though a proud people whose natural inclination is to pull ourselves up by our own bootstraps, we recognize that there is no shame in asking for assistance, especially at a time like this. We stand ready to have discussions with UKG officials to agree on a package of assistance for Anguilla to be provided over the short to medium term. In this regard we were heartened by the expressions of support provided by Foreign Secretary Johnson and Department For International Development Secretary Patel when they visited in the immediate aftermath of Hurricane Irma and look forward to the concrete realization of such pledges. We think that this is an opportune time for the GoA and the UKG to agree on the future of Anguilla and with a crucial element of this being the input of Anguillians to be derived from the Long Term Sustainable Development Plan consultation process. Not to preempt but it would seem that key principles of the Vision for Anguilla going forward would be to build an Inclusive, Resilient, Green and Smart Economy.(2)

It was clear that the chief minister and his cabinet addressed the governor in the most profound manner in a plea to return the island to normalcy. As a result, it became obvious that the talk shows might have misunderstood his plea or made an attempt to politicize the aid needed for the recovery of the island.

Hope began to run high after renowned journalist Keith Stone Graves interviewed the United Kingdom Foreign Secretary Boris Johnson, the governor of Anguilla, His Excellency Tim Foy, and Anguilla's chief minister, Honorable Victor Banks on September 13, 2017 on Radio Anguilla.

Mr. Keith Stone Graves was merciless with his questioning of the foreign secretary. It was very encouraging, however, when the secretary stated that the runway at the airport needed to be extended. He said it was confirmed when the British Air Force aircraft transported him to the island and he was subjected to the sudden halt as it landed. The chief minister used that opportunity to leverage his bargaining power, although one could have easily detected his grief over the Irma disaster. For a moment I thought tears of pain would flow from Chief Minister Banks, as he is ordinarily easily moved to tears, but he unequivocally and uncompromisingly enunciated the sentiments of the Anguillian nationals. He made it clear that there was no need to debate the timing of the British response to the catastrophe and that the people of Anguilla were happy that the British had responded. Chief Minister Banks said there were socioeconomic needs that he called on them to address with expedience, including all the ports of entry; medical, educational and health facilities; and electricity and water. The secretary did not hesitate in agreeing with Chief Minister Banks and promised his commitment and that of the British on every front to return the country to a state of normalcy. However, his promise was not devoid of a level of diplomacy as he continued to praise the Anguillian people for cleaning up the island in the seven days after Hurricane Irma and noting the restoration will be done "together." The word "together" was rather ambiguous.

However, it was felt that the pressure from the international community caused the British Government to respond more favorably to the needs of the battered islands. Particularly, *The Guardian* recorded strong criticism levied against the British by the ex-Attorney General of Anguilla, Rupert Jones, who decried the British for first offering a measly £32 million for all the overseas territories battered by Hurricane Irma.

The article read as follows: "Aid offered by the British government to its hurricane-battered territories in the Caribbean has been dismissed as "derisory" by a former attorney general of one of the worst-hit islands."[3]

The Guardian continued:

Hurricane Irma, now seemingly in its final throes, has shattered Caribbean islands, for which the UK is ultimately responsible. The government now appears to be taking that responsibility more seriously: the foreign secretary, Boris Johnson said he will spend the coming days visiting the British Virgin Islands (BVI) and Anguilla, two of the British dependencies worst hit by Irma. This is beginning to look like an appropriate response.

Until last year, I served as attorney general for Anguilla and my thoughts are with friends and all those who have died or have lost homes and businesses. Media attention will soon move on but the aftermath for many will be grim for months to come: no home, no power, no schools. This will be compounded if the UK's reconstruction effort is not quick and effective. Equally, we must be careful of colonial attitudes to 'victims.' Many of the people who have suffered are resolute and resilient. They have strong spirits and are determined to rebuild quickly.

Many Caribbean islands rely upon tourism; if the airports and hotels are not in a fit state to accept tourists this winter then there will be another blow to their economies. Immediate demands for supplies are one thing, but medium-term infrastructure support is required – we need to know that the electricity and schools are up and running.

The UK government's task is extremely demanding. Yet its commitment so far only to spend £32m in total across the three affected British overseas territories – Anguilla, BVI and Turks and Caicos Islands – is a drop in the Caribbean Sea. Johnson said on Monday that £28m of that has already spent. Are we to believe it will only release a further £4m? This would be derisory – it would not even pay to rebuild one school. I am sure they will do much better. The foreign secretary has also pledged to match taxpayers' donations to the Red Cross. I just hope that we have not arrived at government by crowdfunding.

If this had happened to other UK territories – the Falkland Islands or Gibraltar, for instance – would the response have been the same? To put it in perspective, the government recently spent £285m on St. Helena, its territory in the South Atlantic, for an airport that, sadly, is effectively unusable. The UK's foreign aid budget is around £12bn. There has not yet been any suggestion of other forms of support, such as UK exchange programmes for affected students. Following the volcanic eruptions in the neighbouring territory of Montserrat in the 1990s, two-thirds of the population relocated to the UK. Time will tell what is required.

Of course, the government will claim that it is doing all it can. It will say that troops are on the ground, needs will be met and more money released in due course. To those making unfavourable comparisons with France's response to the crisis, the government may also say the UK does not have direct rule and control over the islands. This is in contrast to the French government's sole responsibility for French St. Martin and St. Barts. But they do accept that the territories are populated by UK citizens and we remain solely responsible for their security and governance. Their founding constitutions are British orders in council – we retain the power to legislate for the territories and in an extreme situations suspend their constitutions and provide for direct rule.

The government's reluctance to commit immediately to deploying significant sums in aid may simply be their huge wheels cranking into gear as they assess the needs to be met. But there are several issues provoked by the relief effort, each of which should spark serious debate about the UK's relationship with its Caribbean overseas territories.

First, does the UK see its partner Caribbean islands as tax havens and secrecy jurisdictions? Some are better known for offshore financial services than tourism. There have been longstanding reports that the islands are havens for corruption, tax avoidance and money laundering. Much of their offshore wealth emanates from the UK. The Panama Papers exposed the level of

BVI ownership of London property. I would hope this publicity would not cause the UK government such embarrassment that it would seek to distance itself from the islands.

Transparency International has done much work highlighting the issues in these offshore jurisdictions. What is less well known is that it was the UK which supported the establishment of these financial outposts in the first place, to benefit and service the city of London.

Legislative attempts to end these secretive arrangements so far have been a fig leaf: last year's compromise agreements fell short of requiring public registries of the beneficial ownership of companies registered in the islands. The economist Richard Murphy has recently called for the donation of any aid from the UK to be conditional on reform of the territories' offshore tax haven status.

The UK may hold the local governments of these territories responsible for these failures. What it does not say is that the UK could legislate to require reform tomorrow if there was the political will. There is not, perhaps, because of the fear that it would highlight the UK's ultimate responsibility. Both UK and local politicians also recognise that the islands' economies, heavily reliant on offshore financial services, might founder with the major loss of jobs.

Then the UK may have to provide alternative investment. It may also rightly believe that the offshore money would simply be moved to other global secrecy jurisdictions.

Second, we should also consider the political situation in each territory. Some local politicians may underplay the help required because they do not want to be seen to cede control to the British government. Some may not want to highlight reliance as they are pushing towards full independence from Britain. Less understandably, they may not want the UK to provide any control or scrutiny of their activities. Some may not want to highlight the extent of the damage for fear of putting off tourists from coming this winter.

Third, we must ask whether it is a priority for the UK government to invest significantly in the territories. The Foreign Office may support a more detached relationship - that of 'partners' rather than former colonial masters. Each territory has its own locally elected government, but is it realistic or fair for these governments to take primary responsibility for such an enormous reconstruction effort? The majority of their citizens still want to maintain a link with the UK, not least for when major assistance is required. If this disaster is not such an occasion, I don't know what is.

Fourth, the government may also have a real concern about controlling to whom aid money will go and how it will be spent. In 2009 the UK temporarily suspended the constitution of the Turks and Caicos, and imposed direct rule following the Auld Commission investigation into alleged governmental corruption. The former premier is currently standing trial and denies all charges. A reported £400m has been spent in Montserrat since the first eruptions of its volcano in 1995, with reported concerns about local mismanagement of aid money.

Finally, the criteria that the Department for International Development uses for aid do not prioritize British overseas territories and their citizens. Eligibility is weighted towards relief for the poorest, regardless of nationality. The territories hit by Hurricane Irma are considered, rightly or wrongly, to be 'middle-income countries' and their populations are not normally eligible for automatic aid. So when the foreign secretary arrives in the Caribbean, I hope he will maximise the UK's response to the devastation wreaked by Irma, as well as using it as an opportunity to discuss our relationship with the overseas territories. It's a conversation long overdue.

It is important to note that some of members of the British Parliament were quick to call out the United Kingdom on its response to the catastrophe. The chairmen, in particular, of the all-party foreign affairs and development select committees, Tom Tugendhat and Stephen Twigg, pleaded for the ministers to explain their response to Irma, warning that people in the UK's overseas territories in the Caribbean remained in grave need.[5]

While the chief minister sought to persuade the populace to view the timing of the United Kingdom's response as immaterial, requesting that all commend them for the fact that they actually arrived, his plea was crowded out by words of condemnation for their sluggish and inadequate response that came even from British MPs.

The British soldiers were very much involved in the cleanup process and sought to assist us in putting our island back together.

Still, the island's essential services, including the Princess Alexandra Hospital, which had lost part of its roof, Anguilla Electricity Company (ANGLEC), with the majority of its electrical poles broken and power lines damaged, and the Water Corporation of Anguilla, with damaged pumps and broken distribution system, all required urgent repairs.

CHAPTER X

MEETING OF THE MINDS

About a week into the aftermath of the Terrorist Hurricane Irma, I was driving along the Stoney Ground Road when my mobile phone rang. Fatigued from the whole ordeal of the disaster, I wearily answered, "Hello, Chris Richardson speaking; who is this?" The caller hesitantly asked, "Chris wey you be?" I recognized Minister Curtis Richardson's voice. He told me he had a question and a request. All who know Minister Richardson would refer to him as very hasty; he abhors procrastination.

His asked abruptly, "Can you put on the water now? The island needs water now and I am telling you to put it on; and come to a meeting with the governor later this afternoon." I immediately reminded him of his request twenty-four hours prior to the storm, when he had demanded that the Water Corporation of Anguilla, of which I was the chairperson, turn the tap on and have water distributed to the entire island against the instructions of the water engineer. The water engineer had given instructions to fill the one-and-a-half-million-gallon (imperial) tank owned by the water corporation and close off the distribution system. This had caused an upset across the island and among the government ministries.

As chairperson, I had met the minister's call to have the pipelines opened before the storm a respectful response, "I am sorry, my board of directors and me have unanimously decided to follow the young engineer's instructions as her rational was scientifically sound." When I had discussed with the water engineer, Kahlea Clifton-James, the possibility of recanting on her decision, she was unyielding, as she claimed the barometric pressure of the storm was falling rapidly and allowing the water level in the tank to fall below twenty-two feet would be catastrophic.

Regarding the minister's question and demand after the passage of the Terrorist Hurricane Irma, I was happy to reiterate that the tank sustained no damage and the water corporation was on a good path to a speedy recovery.

The meeting at government house later that afternoon was a mere fact-finding mission. Many trickled into the meeting late, as its venue was thought to be at the governor's office, while it was at his residence. The three main essential services represented were medical and health, electricity and water. It was clear from the meeting that this event was a baptism of fire for Governor Tim Foy. Anguilla had been his first official appointment as governor in a British overseas territory, and he had been on the job for a period shy of five weeks. He served us soft drinks, mainly water, as his deputy chaired the meeting. I guess he kept any form of alcoholic beverages from the table as that may have caused some to consume beyond the normal in an effort to calm their nerves.

While the water corporation recovery plan was being orchestrated smoothly and efficiently, my acting chief executive officer, water engineer and I did not wish for any intervention that would slow down the process. The governor did mention that one of the resort owners wished to provide complementary water to the water corporation for distribution in a minute area of the island. We considered it a magnificent gesture of a good corporate citizen and my team was quick to embrace the offer; however, we had to soon reject it as the chief minister informed the governor of the caveat that came with the offer. The resort would only provide the water if the water corporation supply this utility to the customers in that area without any charges. This was impractical on many fronts.

The Anguilla Electrical Company (ANGLEC) was deemed in the mire of despair. Their recovery plan at that point in time seemed somewhat vague. It was obvious that their recovery team was overwhelmed by the disaster and the need for outside help was mandatory. This became obvious after much probing from the governor, ministers and the British representative. However, Chief Executive Officer David Gumbs stated clearly the resources he required to complete restoration in three to four months' time. One of the things that stood out at that meeting was the use of bucket trucks to string the lines versus climbers. The commitment was made to do all that was necessary to restore electricity in record time.

The meeting, organized by the Anguilla Hotel Association, was of great interest to many, particularly the hoteliers and industry partners. The attendance was very strong. There were three meetings that happened sequentially; the first was a joint meeting with the members of the Anguilla Hotel Association, the second with the chairlady of the Anguilla Tourist Board and the third with Chief Minister Victor Banks, Parliamentary Secretary Cordigan Connor and Permanent Secretary Larry Franklyn. The chief minister's segment of the meeting was most exciting.

When the minister and his team arrived, the relief was likened to patients waiting in an emergency room and seeing the doctor arrive. The session was conducted informally without a set agenda. It was obvious the stakeholders were looking to government for answers relating to the public relations Anguilla was doing with the outer world and the restoration of the electricity supply. On the other hand, the chief minister was anxious to learn of the damages their properties sustained and their reopening time frame.

Many of the properties seemed hopeful that they could return to full operation within the hotel season after the festive season of 2017. It was made clear by very few of the resorts' representatives that January 2018 was a more feasible date under consideration for reopening.

As a hospitality practitioner it was troubling for me and I questioned in my mind if the properties would really open after the festive season. It is important to note that guests would have paid for their stay months in advance in order to secure their reservations. Christmas (festive) is a very critical period of the tourist season as it accounts for the bulk of revenues the properties earn for the tourist season. As a matter of fact, one could have almost been certain that most of these properties would have already utilized these deposits to meet their recurrent expenditures during the summer period when guests' arrivals are extremely low. Hence, I was not shocked to hear property owners trying to drum up a consensus to retain these deposits for future stays, particularly the following festive season. This plea was ignored to the displeasure of the proponents.

The chief minister was very positive and assured the hoteliers that the Government of Anguilla would do everything possible to have the properties up and running within record time.

The silence was deafening. It was obvious they might have been doubting the chief minister's commitment. They all left the meeting with different ideas; some of these ideas might soon be implemented to the detriment of the local hotel staff.

Meeting of the Minds

CHAPTER XI

DISLOYALTY MET
WITH LOYALTY

A few days after the Anguilla Hotel Association meeting, I received a call from a
colleague at one of the five-star properties on the island and she asked my opinion of the
meeting. I didn't wish to reveal my thoughts as
they were less than acceptable; however, I decided
I would give her an optimistic sneak peek of what
was going on in my head. She, too, was fearful that
the season would be a stressed one for all the
properties and the decisions of hotel owners
would bear down heavily on the staff.

Before the storm, Cap Juluca had announced
its closure for the entire tourist season, September

2017 to November 2018. The company sought to redeploy its staff at other Belmont properties during the interim period. Some of the staff members were reluctant to travel to distant lands and began sorting through other options on the island. Some were placed at La Samana, a five-star resort on French St. Martin, but unfortunately this property sustained damages from Hurricane Irma requiring at least twelve months of repairs. The staff at this property initially was not in despair, as they were apprised in advance of the resort's temporary closure. However, a few months into the aftermath of Hurricane Irma, the La Samana staff saw a disingenuous side exhibited by the ownership of this property.

Four Seasons Resort and Residences Anguilla sustained mammoth damages and stated clearly that they could not receive guests in less than six months from the date of the storm. Many suspected that the resort would have to release their staff on the basis of their contractual employment arrangement, but they proved otherwise. As the resort manages many properties world-wide, they made offers to many of their staff members to have them placed at various properties, including Nevis in the Caribbean and Canada. Many of the staff members remained and assisted with the cleaning up of the resort and its reconstruction. Many of the nationals complimented this resort for its commitment to its staff even at a time when revenues were not being generated.

Further, Four Seasons Resort operated a full-service lunch restaurant complimentary to all employees. This was widely commended.

Malliouhana Hotel at Auberge was said to have received minimal damage. As the attack on this resort by Hurricane Irma, the Terrorist, happened during the hotel's two-month annual maintenance period, it was projected that it would reopen its doors for guests by November 1st, 2017. Many of the staff members were optimistic that the property would open in record time and they held to this implicit promise.

From all appearances the damages were minimal and the staff observed it. But their sense of job security lasted for a fleeting moment. Staff members were soon informed that the damages were more than what had met the eye and the property would be closed for an extended period of time, with a possible reopen date in April, 2018. The staff was promised reduced wages until that time. It was not the short time away from full employment the staff expected but they thought it was best to allow patience to prevail.

The assertion that the property would reopen in April, 2018 soon seemed unrealistic. While some of the debris had been removed from the property, much of the effects of the storm were clearly evident. Four months after the passage of the storm, the white entrance "hut" to the resort was slanted at about a twenty-degree angle, the roof of the canteen was exposed with no signs of repairs taking place and the tennis courts remained in a decrepit manner.

While the meager wages were paid irregularly, the staff members anticipated a brighter day and continued to serve diligently. It became most disheartening to many that four months after the storm the resort retained its director of operations, executive chef, sous chef and director of finance.

These positions reportedly received full salaries although they were unable to perform their functions as dictated by their job descriptions. This irked the nationals indeed.

CuisinArt Golf Resort and Spa suffered extensive damages from the storm. Its sister property, The Reef at CuisinArt, received damages to its towering building. This structure, viewed as an edifice that is out of sync with Anguilla's tourist properties, seemingly sustained severe damages compared with Malliouhana at Auberge, yet they had set a reopen date of April 2018.

Cuisinart Golf Resort and Spa and The Reef at CuisinArt are both owned by the same owner, Mr. Leandro Rizzuto. The Golf Resort and Spa sustained major damage to its physical structure and the coastline. The breakfast and lunch restaurant, a customized fabric structure, was in the center of the property. It was enjoyed by many guests due to its location. This structure was tossed all over the resort and became a main debris field along with the hotel's hydroponics farm structure. It was expected that the landscaping would have been annihilated. Some of the plants were spared, but the property, on viewing immediately after the storm, was not an encouraging sight; it looked like a war zone.

This property was originally opened on December 20, 1999 and the staff turnover is very low. The owner of the property fostered a family environment in the earlier years and this spirit of belongingness continued. I learned that many were tearful when they observed the destruction. The owner promised the staff through his vice-president and general manager that he would retain them and sought to provide employment during the closure of the resort. The hours were reduced but as many said, "half of loaf is better than none." The wages may have been meager but it demonstrated a great level of care. It is important to note that the owner did not use the insurance business interruption policy to disadvantage his staff. Actually, it was said that the property was "self-insured."

Some of the staff at other resorts were not as fortunate. It was a sad event at Zemi Beach House as the staff were herded into the bar area of the property to hear their fate. The azure water at which the staff gazed that morning seemed like the Dead Sea; the superficial damages were hardly obvious to the naked eye. As they waited for the owner, the general manager and human resource director, one could have heard a pin drop. There was utter silence. The nervous whispers made it clear that the staff feared the worst; they were all concerned about their jobs and the chatter throughout the island did not suggest a good ending.

When the owner and his entourage arrived, they were received with mixed emotions. He offered his usual pleasantries and his facial expression preceded his message of doom. He informed all that due to the storm the resort was unable to continue to function and as a result all contracts would be terminated. Many looked at him in bewilderment and disbelief. When the floor was open for questions a few staff asked about the employer-employee loyalty. The owner was calm and tried his best to deliver the message as gently as possible but there is no easy way of telling someone they are fired even though it was aggravated through no fault of their own but a storm.

The staff looked like they were standing in an inferno as the sweat of despair and agony poured down their faces on that cool Tuesday morning of October 3rd, 2017. I was really sorry for both staff and owner.

While the physical damages to the resort may have seemed miniscule, the island's devastated infrastructure could not support the resort being opened for the festive season 2017. There were no answers as to the reopening of the resort. The pain on the faces was evident; many questioned their acts of loyalty.

While most of the resorts tried to provide some form of hope to their employees, the level of communication between management of Zemi Beach House and staff was less than acceptable as time progressed. Most were left wondering about their fate.

CHAPTER XII

THE FACES

The Anguilla Red Cross and other donor agencies made themselves available in the relief effort for the people of Anguilla. Many questioned the efforts of the Red Cross on the ground and their judgement in the distribution of relief items. In small societies like ours, it is not uncommon for aspersions to be made by those who view themselves to be marginalized by the system. Needless to say, the Red Cross' acts of possible goodwill were tried and judged in the public domain.

I did receive calls from guests overseas who wished to make donations and inquired of a possible conduit via which such donations could be made; however, they declined to use the Red Cross. After carefully researching this global organization, I realized its reputation may have been considered questionable in many circles. However, Blanchards Restaurant on the island soon created a fund to provide additional meaningful supplies to the nationals of the island.

The Blanchards, a husband and wife team, have been on the island for at least three decades. They were the founding partners for the Mango's Restaurant at West End, which they sold many years ago when they began Blanchards Restaurant, a haute cuisine facility at Meads Bay. They have always worked closely with their staff at the restaurant and developed a family environment. Hence, it was easy for them to identify the needs of the island and set about establishing a fund that raised hundreds of thousands of dollars. It was purported that it was properly structured and many guests of Anguilla, mostly citizens of the United States of America, made sizable contributions to it.

The Blanchards provided relief items to Anguillians with limited restrictions. The islanders were excited to receive generators that would supply homes with some form of electricity, and chainsaws and other tools that would make it easy for the trimming of trees and getting the island back to normalcy quickly. The islanders were really thrilled with the excellent corporate citizen spirit which the Blanchards exhibited.

A team, which involved the participation of Mr. Thomas Kelly, organized a relief effort out of the United States of America. They provided forty-foot ocean containers. Mr. Kelly's mother is one of Anguilla's outstanding teachers and was principal at a school that Anguilla renamed in her honor, The Teacher Orelia Kelly Primary School. The pride of Anguillians was evident when they received bags of rice on which was written, "Feed the starving children." The noise of disgust soon spread throughout the island. I was sitting in a meeting with government ministers and parastatal representatives when one of the members raised the complaint of the residents regarding the label on the rice. Actually, most of the persons in the meeting grabbed a packet with the hope of providing the necessary feedback. Most found the rice to be of excellent taste and quality. The Anguillians were soon convinced by the ministers of government that the label on the rice had not infringed on its excellent nutritional value as inscribed on the packet. However, there were many other items Mr. Kelly's team made available and were gladly received by the nationals. Actually, Mr. Kelly had always been considered the ultimate informal ambassador of Anguilla and his act of benevolence was well received by to all.

The spirit of giving from our Caribbean neighbors was tremendous. We excitedly took our telescope on the Back Street of South Hill and witnessed boats from Monserrat, St. Christopher (St. Kitts) and Nevis and other countries gracing our shores with water and various food supplies. Further, it brought tears of joy to the eyes of many when a ship arrived from the Dominican Republic carrying containers of fresh produce and fruits, dairy products and meats. The first of the many loads were trucked to the Christian Fellowship Church at Blowing Point Road for distribution. I was extremely tired from the whole ordeal of the aftermath of the storm over the weeks but I quickly regained my energy when my telephone rang and learned it was Minister Curtis Richardson on the line requesting my assistance in the distribution of such food supplies.

"The Anguilla Stronger" organization was an effort by four of the five major resorts on the island, created with good intentions, but which experienced extended delays. It was purported that they raised in excess of $1 million (US) but the mechanism had various hiccups. It was made clear that no monies would be presented to any of the staff members from the four resorts, but that it would go for building materials and food supplies. However, there was the expectation from many that there would have been a flow of goods and services into the island in record time.

There was a gentleman we affectionately called "Speedy" who worked at one of the resorts and was excited by the fact that he was informed by the owner of the property where he worked that it was possible that his roof, which he lost during the Terrorist Hurricane Irma, would be restored. He had been bequeathed a little house by his grandmother, approximately fifteen feet wide and sixteen feet long. Its walls were constructed with cinder blocks joined by four concrete columns at its four corners, and the roof had a gable design made of treated pine wood and galvanized metal sheets. This house had meant the world to him and his meager income was insufficient to replace the roof. Moreover, his services were terminated from the property where he worked due to Hurricane Irma, which was in line with the Fair Labor Standards Act, and he received two weeks' severance payment. This may have been enough money to purchase only a couple sheets of galvanized metal sheets. Hence, he trusted that the "Anguilla Stronger" construction would have come to his rescue in a timely manner but he was to be disappointed.

I was sitting on the beach during dusk on a Friday, enjoying a beautiful sunset, when my mobile phone vibrated. Gazing at the sun going down on the horizon, I was not prepared for any form of distraction. However, I happened to glance at my phone almost at the ending of the ring and realized it was Speedy. I quickly gave in to the distraction and answered fondly, expecting good news from him. He asked if the material for the roofing had been disbursed by the "Anguilla Stronger" organization. I informed him that I was unsure and gave him the number and contact person. I heard the pain of loss and the anguish in his voice. He continued, "Chris, it is hard, I have lost much but I hope to regain it all." I recognized he was hopeful as tears streamed down my face, blurring the beauty of a Friday evening sunset.

I got on the phone, made a few calls and contacted Speedy within ten minutes to inform him that the distribution logistics were still a work in progress. I heard the anxiety in his sighing.

Finally, one morning I heard a gentle rap on the door of my home, and to my surprise, it was "Speedy." He had stopped by to let me know he was able to purchase enough material to restore his house, as he had accepted a job which paved the way for his restoration. That meant the world to me. He left a message with me that day that will remain in my memory for the remainder of my life, "Disappointment is not the gateway to despondency, but a turnpike to a plethora of opportunities." His willpower was not damaged by his disappointment, it was only bolstered.

Many, however, benefited from the "Anguilla Stronger" organization despite its many delays and setbacks. It proved itself to be a strong support to the hotel workers and their families, socially, economically and otherwise. I tried on a few occasions to visit the kitchen of Four Seasons Resort where meals had been prepared on designated days of the week for the villagers and other hotel workers but was unsuccessful. From all reviews the meals were excellent and were prepared by well-qualified chefs.

CHAPTER XIII

THE FIREBALL

Chief Minister Bank's optimistic visit to the United Kingdom on February 17th, 2018, was discussed in the February 13th, 2018, executive council's meeting. The discussion at this meeting was centered around securing funding in order to restore the island to normalcy. With unemployment going through the ceiling and little revenue adding to the government's coffers, this was of great concern to government. The chief minister was adamant that he would not declare Anguilla a failed state, contrary to the opposition's sentiments.

A clipping from the executive council's meeting demonstrated the desire of Governor Tim Foy and Chief Minister Banks to return the island to normalcy following a few months of reconstruction, along with a glimmer of hope from the tourism sector.

Governor Foy was pleased that the chief minister was paying an early visit to the Foreign and Commonwealth Office in London and stated, "He will be discussing the sixty-million pounds sterling grant and the conditions for its release. I think that the work on that is very well advanced, and is moving quite quickly. It is good that the chief got an early opportunity to have a conversation around that matter."

Beside the sixty million pounds sterling, the governor expressed his sentiments regarding smaller sums of funding that were being made available for repairs of infrastructure, like the Rodney MacArthur Rey Auditorium that would enable students at the Comprehensive School to take their examinations in a comfortable setting. He added, "I think we can now turn a leaf on Irma, and begin to look forward to the positive things for the future because there are lots and lots to do."

Following Governor Foy's comments, Chief Minister Banks stated categorically, "We have turned the corner on the recovery effort and I think that the key issue is that we have secured some financing – not only the sixty-million he referred to – but we are constantly picking at the UK Conflict Security and Stability Fund and getting other benefits from it. I am very happy that the Governor's Office has been able to assist us in moving that forward for some critical projects. Having the Rodney MacArthur Rey Auditorium in preparedness for the examinations has been an area of great concern to me, as well as to having a plan in place to restore stability to the Albena Lake-Hodge Comprehensive School. Restoring the school is one of the most important issues that I consider we have to deal with from a social sector standpoint."

He continued, "The sixty million pounds sterling will finance a number of schools and will also deal with access to Anguilla at the terminal buildings both on this island and on the Dutch side of St. Maarten. We are focusing on access very comprehensively because we want to make sure that the visitor experience coming out of Juliana, which has its own challenges, can be mitigated. We have had some meetings with key hoteliers in the upper end of the tourism industry about other issues including the big issue of the Labour Code. In those discussions the hoteliers pointed out the importance of getting something done about access to Anguilla."

The chief minister also spoke about the importance and urgency of getting a number of infrastructure projects in a state of managerial readiness in anticipation of the release of the sixty million pounds sterling from the U.K. government in April 2018. He emphasized, "As the governor mentioned, I am going to the U.K. on Saturday. The delegation will include my permanent secretary, Dr. Aidan Harrigan, as well as the deputy governor who has been actively involved in the recovery process in the aftermath of Hurricane Irma. I think it is important that we have a team which can respond to all the issues."

The chief minster was confident that the mother country would meet its commitment; he was adamant that Britain's Prime Minister Theresa May's decision to grant the sixty million pounds sterling in aid would be dispensed in record time. This assurance was borne out of the meeting held in the United Kingdom along with other distressed British Overseas Territories seeking aid likewise.

Chief Minister Banks received a heroic welcome from his supporters on his return from the United Kingdom, as word of his successes in his meeting with the British Officials had preceded his return. An ardent supporter and enthusiast of the Anguilla United Front, the incumbent political party headed by Banks, taunted the opposition by stating, "Only Banks coulda bring home de bacon," The naysayers were infuriated and responded, "We want more than bacon, we want beef." On every street corner discussion intensified as the islanders expressed their distrust over the British commitment to assist the destitute islands which included the British Virgin Islands and the Turks and Caicos Islands in particular. I recalled engaging in one of these discussions at Ken's BBQ Grill in The Valley, as I was willing to believe Chief Minister Banks' visit to the United Kingdom was a success story. However, one of the ladies in the group said, "The longer we look back in history the further we will see in the future." She continued, "Goddamn it, the British got no integrity; history has proven dem to be liars and to hell with dem. Banks will not even get to smell the bacon; independence is the path to take."

High-profile meetings were held at the ministerial level as to the disbursement of the funds. As chairman of the Water Corporation, I was at a meeting of the executive council on a matter regarding the Water Corporation when Governor Tim Foy interjected, "Chris, I must have a word with you because the Water Corporation is going to get a portion of the sixty million pounds sterling for infrastructural purposes; I will meet with you and the minister." I became elated and remained in wait for the meeting.

A list of the projects was named as being attached to the sixty million pounds sterling but dreams were soon shattered when it was noised abroad that the British were placing stipulations on the disbursement of the funds. The radio stations and the political pundits, particularly from the opposition, began taking the government to task. It was the expectation of the electorate that the opposition would join forces with the government in an effort to ensure that funding flow to Anguilla in a timely manner; however, the divisiveness was palpable. Rumors began to spread that Anguillians were leaving the island in droves and going to the United Kingdom in search of work as Anguilla's economic future was becoming more abysmal.

The chief minister quickly defended his position that the island had not been experiencing any mass migration as purported by some of the private radio stations. Not many days after his assertion, the chief minister revealed a letter to the public from Lord Ahmad placing demands on his administration before the funding could be released.

The battles for the chief minister were real and they were fierce; having no defined press secretary in place allowed the radio talk shows to take center stage and divulge information at will. Some of the information carried a certain measure of authenticity while other pieces of information were merely preposterous and politically driven.

The Fireball

CHAPTER XIV

ANGUILLA STRONGER MAYHEM

The Government of Anguilla granted a duty-free concession to all who assisted the island by providing relief items. Many vehicles were driven with broken windscreens and houses were without roofs and windows. It was generous of the government to grant the duty-free concession but it was the view of many that the administrative fee should have been waived as well.

Many persons took advantage of this concession; I really believe the insurance companies were relieved as this reduced their payouts tremendously. The process was another matter; this was obvious as some of the customs officers were not aware of the processing procedures of such a concession. Nonetheless, it was an excellent gesture by the government, which no one denied. There were those persons who were dissatisfied, as they expected the government to include other imported items on the duty-free concession list.

I attended a town hall meeting in early January 2018 and many questions were raised regarding the concession. I recall a gentleman stating that he had some damages to his house and whilst he got duty-free concession on the doors, the concession did not include the locks or varnish for the doors. The audience sighed in disgust as they thought he was pushing for too much. At that point a lady with a strong British accent rose from her seat and reminded all that in life there are no free lunches. She cautioned that whilst the British consented to the duty-free concession, we would eventually pay for such through increased taxes or other means. There was a hush over the auditorium and many began to ponder her statement as it really struck home. The British gave nothing without a price tag. A few weeks after the meeting, in an effort to ensure as many persons as possible took advantage of the duty-free concession, the government extended the concession for an additional three months.

There were organizations expecting an open-ended concessionary policy. Seven months into the aftermath of the Terrorist, Hurricane Irma, one of the donor groups fired a missile of angry words at the Government of Anguilla in defense of requests it made to government without a reasonable response. I was sitting in a meeting on a Sunday morning in early May of 2018, when I got a text message on my mobile phone. I was hesitant to open it but I soon surrendered to the temptation and observed a letter from "Anguilla Stronger," which seemingly was circulated to its members. The letter, in essence, called for a protest against the Government of Anguilla's decision to apply customs duty on relief items. It was direct and was a rabble-rousing instrument. The letter sent shock waves through the entire island. Having sent the letter to their members allowed Anguilla Stronger to reach the hands of the opposition and it ignited a political firestorm.

A native Anguillian who currently resides overseas posted on his Facebook page, "Beware of the Greeks bearing gifts." In another post I read, "Bob Marley said in a song, 'And when you're going to get some food, your brother got to be your enemy.'" The divisiveness between the opposition and government widened bitterly as the main opposition party, Anguilla United Movement (AUM), like a dog to a bone, held to this letter and used it as a political weapon. The letter was reposted on the Facebook page of one of the AUM candidates with the party's comment, "A government that lacks empathy in times of need is a government that has grown arrogant. This letter demonstrates the sort of inaction and lack of compassion the Anguilla United Front has showed since Hurricane Irma."

Whilst the radio stations made their comments, the social media platforms had a field day over the letter. There were those nationals who supported the correspondence and many expressed their disappointment at the very thought of the author or authors of the letter. Many questioned the very intention of it and thought it was orchestrated by the opposition.

Chief Minister Banks allowed the nine-day story to sizzle and, like a scud missile, he shot back with a press release:

Fellow Anguillians,

Many Anguillians may have read a press circular on social media from the Anguilla Stronger Emergency Relief Fund in connection with its decision to curtail its relief program to a number of Anguillians who have been recipients of these contributions since October 2017 in the aftermath of the infamous Hurricane Irma. The gist of the circular is that the decision to curtail the relief program is as a result of Government not fulfilling its commitment to exempt the Fund from normal Customs duties.

Let me say at the outset that the Government and People of Anguilla strongly applaud The Starwood Capital Group for initiating this Fund and bringing on Board the other major hotel properties on the island to participate. I can recall the passion with which Mr. Roy Shanholtz, Vice President, Starwood Capital presented the idea to Government --- as well as the efforts he employed to advance it from concept to reality. And I sincerely and gratefully commend the entire organization for its contribution to the cause of relief and restoration during the traumatic and depressing period after Irma. Anguillians will forever acknowledge this debt of gratitude for your contribution.

And while I am on my feet, let me also thank the literally hundreds of donors, many of which have asked to remain anonymous, for their support during those challenging times. This list includes investors in Anguilla; friends of Anguilla overseas; the Anguillian Diaspora groups and organizations; and countries and institutions from the region and the wider world community. Anguillians feel proud for the respectful manner in which these various individuals and groups have engaged us in the relief and recovery process. We felt that this came from a genuine sense of charity devoid of any form of indignity or humiliation. No fanfare or boastfulness!

It is not my intention to engage the Management of Anguilla Stronger on any issues regarding the slow progress of the resolution of the issues regarding its importations --- clearly there may be fair criticisms about the pace of that bureaucracy. However, we must express our dissatisfaction with the manner in which the Executive Director of Anguilla Stronger, in particular, has been engaging officials of the Anguilla Government. While I thank the Executive Director for her hard work, zeal and dedication, many recipients of her emails have expressed the view that they find her approach to be rude, disrespectful, and condescending.

These officials also believe that anyone upon reading her correspondence to Senior Government officials would come to a similar conclusion. Needless to say, there are many officials who feel offended by the accusatory nature of some of the statements in the correspondence. Some of those statements would suggest that Government is extorting money from Anguilla Stronger and putting it to uses other than for the benefit of the people of Anguilla.

There are clear protocols about the management of relief, recovery, and reconstruction that apply in the aftermath of any disaster in Anguilla. This is to avoid the chaos that can result from having several well-intentioned donors eager to assist. There is a period for relief; there is a period for recovery; and there is a period for reconstruction. As far as these periods are concerned, Government is required to make certain determinations with regards timing after reviewing the entire situation. They granted concessions for foodstuffs up until December 14, 2017; and building materials, etc., up until March 31, 2018.

Rightly or wrongly, we believe it was necessary to establish timelines guided by the fact that businesses in Anguilla also need to carry on their operations and must at some point be able to sell their products on which they have paid Customs duty. That Customs duty goes to pay for Government services for all the people of Anguilla which includes education, health, community development, police, fire services, and so on.

Customs duties constitute more than 40% of our revenue in an economy where there are no personal or corporate taxes. I must also mention that it is not the practice to give duty-free concessions on consumables -- this only applies during such disasters and other very, very, deserving cases. In fact, the whole concept of bringing in relief is based on situations where the availability of such items has been affected by the disaster because of limitations on imports.

Having said all that, there is absolutely no reason why Anguilla Stronger should not be treated in a special way -- given the nature of the organization and the genuine intentions of its donors/contributors. But we can have an objective discussion about that in an atmosphere of mutual respect. There is absolutely no value in veiled threats and derogatory statements. We are all on the same team. And we respect and appreciate the "widow's mite" as readily as we respect and appreciate the "largesse" from donors of great means.

The latest circular of May 4, 2018 has clearly crossed the line in terms of the manner in which persons or organizations coming into our country to assist in times of natural disaster should conduct themselves. The circular clearly enters the realm of local politics by making statements that can bring the duly elected Government into disrepute and further tries to mobilize the recipients of relief against the Government.

For those listeners who have not read or seen the circular, let me highlight a few deprecating statements that were included in the circular and then explain why we consider them offensive. The author of the circular said and I quote:

"And while we were busy delivering to you, your Government was busy taking from you."

This clearly implies that the Government is actually taking away money from needy Anguillans.

"(They) trusted us to be good guardians of their donations, ensuring no dollar was ever wasted."

This suggests that paying customs duty is a waste. Maybe the author believes that all that Anguillians need to make it after Irma is the benevolence of Anguilla Stronger.

"We want to believe your Government is committed to helping the people of Anguilla."

This questions whether this Government is truly committed to the people they represent as much as Anguilla Stronger purports to be. This is blatantly self-righteous to say the least.

"At the root of our core mission is love. Love for Anguilla. Love for you, the people of Anguilla who make a naturally beautiful island extraordinarily special. And love for helping you and others in any way we can."

This comes across very mushy. We do believe that Anguilla Stronger loves the people of Anguilla and have been very generous. However, the context suggests that they love Anguilla more than the duly elected Government and have their interests more at heart.

"Please share your testimonials with us so that we can share it with your Government."

Soliciting statements on how much the natives appreciate them, could appear as if the author of this circular has intentions to run for political office in Anguilla.

Let me make a few candid points in terms of the way we feel. Anguillians appreciate the support and relief provided by generous donors but at the end of the day we are proud people and do not want to be dependent on baskets of food indefinitely. Anguillians want to get jobs and business opportunities so that they can fend for themselves and their families, not handouts.

They want a fair day's wage for a fair day's pay -- not to be on contract without the guarantee of long-term employment to bring stability into their lives and security at the bank.

They want to have labour laws that protect them against ruthless employers — not to operate in an employment relationship where the rules are not clear.

They want to be able to aspire to the highest echelons of management in their country not to be passed over simply because they are not perceived to be qualified. In a few words: "They want a hand up, not a handout!"

It is in this context, that the idea of the author of the circular telling us how much their organization has done for the country can come across as being very patronizing -- giving the impression that they care more about you than your own representatives care about you. It gives the impression that the author derives a sense of power having Anguillians in this charitable relationship for extended periods of time.

We, too, have testimonials from Anguillians who feel that it is demeaning to be standing in line seven months after Irma to get a basket of food from Anguilla Stronger. Many persons who actually need the assistance do not show up. This is why the Government has suggested that perhaps vouchers or cash as we have done is a more dignified way of assisting seven months after the storm. People then can buy with dignity what they actually need. Not what someone believes they deserve. In addition, businesses in Anguilla who pay customs duty can make a sale and keep their businesses viable.

What I am saying is that this requires a civil exchange and discussion among all parties concerned. And if the contributors understand the philosophy of what is appropriate at this time I am sure that Anguilla Stronger can convince them that this approach will be more universally helpful.

I am not sure exactly who the author or authors of this circular are. However, I firmly believe that the contents of that document do not reflect the views of the donors of Anguilla Stronger. They would not expect their team operating in a jurisdiction outside of their borders, would conduct themselves in such a manner. I would think that they would be extremely upset to have any officer in their organization engaging with their host Government in such a blatantly divisive and political tone.

As Chief Minister of Anguilla I will always treat investors and visitors to our island with mutual respect. I will be meeting with some of the principals of Anguilla Stronger over the next few days to personally voice my dissatisfaction with the tone of the circular. This approach to our negotiations is clearly unwarranted.

I therefore look forward to a meeting that can establish the kind of relationship that can lead to a better environment in which to advance the interest of the Anguillian people. Although we have different roles I am sure that we are on the same team -- no individual or group of individuals have the monopoly on the best way to make Anguilla stronger, better, and more resilient. And most of all we want the world to recognize that it is our purpose to build a nation proud, strong, and free. You may have noticed that in that mantra "proud" comes first.

May God bless you all and may God Bless Anguilla.

The subtle but profound tone with which he delivered this address was welcomed by many who viewed Chief Minister Banks as a statesman, one who has used silence more often than not as a means of responding to his critics.

The following day I walked into a store and overheard a conversation among two elderly couples. One person said, "Aya Lard, I always knew Wictor had balls, but I didn't know he had teeth. It was damned well full time he put dem people in dey place, we may want de morsel but don't throw it in we face."

While the chief minister's critics continued to apply political pressure based on the letter, his response brought clarity to many of the nationals and in general he was viewed as being heroic.

Despite the saga, Anguilla Stronger continued on to present movie nights for the nationals on the Saturday evening following the press release.

Actually, the relief supplies were reinstated by Anguilla Stronger and the nationals gladly continued to take full advantage of this offering.

Nature's Terrorist Hurricane Irma

CHAPTER XV

"A HAND BEGETS ANOTHER"

The island seemed rather dismal for both the Thanksgiving period and the festive season 2017. The supporting arms of the hospitality industry all were asleep.

On occasions I visited the taxi stations at the two main ports, Clayton Lloyd International Airport and Blowing Point. There was a deep level of anxiety among many of the taxi drivers. The discussions were very interesting and centered around politics. It has always been said that our main sport is boat racing but I find that has long since changed. The passion with which Anguillians discuss boat racing is incomparable to that of politics. However, the taxi drivers take the lead over that of the radio talk shows when discussing politics. But, on this particular day, I decided to sit under the temporary tent that housed the taxi drivers during the waiting period. A discussion ensued about Anguilla's former industries and one of the taxi drivers who many consider conceited raised the issue about selfishness and the need for Anguillians to get together and rebuild.

He claimed that he had worked some years prior with a rock crusher owner who had a hydraulic dump truck, which was a unique feature for a truck of the 1960s. During that period, rocks and sand were loaded onto the trucks by hand shovels and off-loaded using the same method. The owner, Mr. Webster, cared for his truck and didn't give any credence to hitchhikers' signals. He was adamant that having an extra person on the truck would increase his fuel bill, and the fuel was just enough for the chauffeur.

One day he was driving from his home in Island Harbor to The Valley, the central town of Anguilla, in his truck and a hitchhiker signaled him for a ride; it was his usual practice to drive not more than fifteen miles per hour, which made it easy for him to look out of the window and reply verbally, "I only have petrol in the truck for one person and it has one person in it already and that is me, sorry." The hitchhiker knew him quite well as they were friendly neighbors. However, he walked on and a half an hour later he saw the baby blue-colored truck at the road side and Mr. Webster standing beside it, looking bereft with his hands on his hips. The young man looked across at the truck, observed he had a punctured front tire and jeered at Mr. Webster by saying, "Could you believe a two-wheeled human being can overtake a six-wheeler? I made history today." Mr. Webster chuckled in embarrassment and beckoned him, "I am having some back pain and this old man is having it hard jacking up this truck. Can you give me a hand?" The man replied, "This two-wheeled human being only have enough food to walk it to The Valley, I am sorry I cannot help." Mr. Webster replied, "Don't worry about walking I am going to the same place and can take you." The man responded, "Have you put more fuel in your truck? I am afraid the next thing will happen is that you run out of fuel before we reach The Valley, then I will have to walk to The Valley carrying you on my shoulders." That response angered Mr. Webster.

The hitchhiker went on his merry way, leaving Mr. Webster to deal with his punctured tire. He was left to change his tire on a sick back, which was not good for him at all. The taxi driver who relayed the story stated, "Lend a hand and you get hearts in exchange."

Another taxi driver shared the story of a gentleman who lived in St. Thomas many years ago and had a prominent job with the federal government. He was an Anguillian by birth but as a teenager he migrated to St. Thomas for a better way of life. He carried the alias "Cleanman." He was given that name because his deportment was impeccable and he was easily spotted in a crowd with an envious height, charming features and suave countenance. Cleanman drove a brightly colored Volkswagen car and in those days owning a car at his age portrayed economic progress. One would have observed his car on the road from a distance due to its distinct color. But he was quite an aloof gentleman and had very few friends. Every time he was seen in his car he was all alone. Many were cautioned not to engage in hitchhiking any rides in his car as there were no seats in the back and he allowed no one to sit in the front of the car with him. One day two guys decided to ignore the warnings and decided to ask Cleanman for a ride in his two-door Volkswagen. He delightfully consented but the guys couldn't get the door open and had to decline his offer.

One day Cleanman's car was taken to the mechanic shop for repairs and it was noted that the passenger door had been soldered tight by him in an effort not to give anyone a ride in his car. Eventually, life seemingly was unkind to him, as he lost his job, his car and eventually his home. Poetic justice had taken its toll on Cleanman as he walked the streets and "begged his bread." He received little sympathy and eventually was taken off the street and died in a home, lonely and destitute.

The cabdriver admonished, "Sharing is caring and this is the time for us to share with each other or our life story will end like Cleanman."

Nature's Terrorist Hurricane Irma

CHAPTER XVI

THE SHELTERS' DILEMMA

My son asked me a pointed question during the storm. "Dad, there are human shelters but what happen to all the animals that walk the streets without owners?" It was a question I was unable to answer. However, it struck me that we are not truly animal-friendly. I told him of my childhood days when rats were caught in the rat traps and we were summoned to bury them in the backyard. We held ceremonies with one of us acting like the priest and committed their bodies to the ground with the maxim, "Ashes to ashes, dust to dust."

During Hurricane Irma, some persons untied their goats and allowed them to roam; many tried to strengthen their sheep and goat holding pens, hoping they would stand against the fury of the storm. I was later informed that the Animal Shelter did provide a safe haven for those animals without homes. However, many persons were so preoccupied in securing their families that animals were last on their list in the scheme of things.

The selected human shelters across the island were chosen based on their perceived structural strength and resilience to hurricane-force winds. Such buildings were designated for the sheltering of persons whose personal dwelling houses were cited as being unsafe in times of storms of a certain magnitude. The buildings were examined by qualified personnel working with the Anguilla Disaster Preparedness Division supported by our local qualified engineers. Over the years, it has been customary for many of the churches or associated buildings and schools to be designated as shelters.

Obviously, it is expected that the roofs, windows, doors, walls and foundations of these buildings could withstand at least a Category Five hurricane. A hurricane of this magnitude, Hurricane

Irma, was expected to have sustained winds of at least 185 miles per hour and gusts peaking at 225 miles per hour. I often wonder why some of these selected buildings have galvanized metal sheeted roofing. On second thought, it was my view that the designations were made only as a matter of policy. Anguilla is being called a country but indeed we live like a hamlet; we live as a loving community. Everyone knows each other and it is easy to believe that some of us would use our houses as shelters for our neighbors should the need arise.

The West End shelter, the Alwyn Allison Richardson Primary School Auditorium, was used as a secured hurricane shelter and from all appearances it looked rather sturdy. Actually, it was one of the more modern shelters being staffed by officers from the Anguilla Fire Department. The building was slammed by Hurricane Irma, leaving a trail of damage totaling approximately $231,000 (US). It is worth mentioning that all the shelters sustained damages but not as severe as the West End shelter. The estimated damages to all five designated shelters, per the assessment by the Disaster Preparedness Unit, was $305,400 (US).

In the wee hours of the morning, as Hurricane Irma began edging in on the western part of the island, there was a sense of security felt by the West End community. Earlier the previous day, the police and firefighters had made their way through the village and admonished those who were in seemingly unsafe homes to move to the shelter. Some were reluctant to do so and only sought shelter after their houses were decapitated by the Terrorist, Hurricane Irma. One of the houses that required evacuation during the storm had as its occupant a lady who was approximately seven months pregnant.

As Digicel, the mobile telephone service provider, lost its service at the immediate beginning of the storm, the three firefighters who staffed the shelter had no means of communication, as they all had only Digicel service. One of the neighbors of the shelter, having FLOW telecommunication services, was contacted by the Disaster Preparedness Unit informing her that they were unable to make contact with the shelter and requested of her an update. Looking out of her key peephole she observed the firefighters moving from one building to the next on the school compound. Her caring spirit didn't allow her to recline back into her easy chair. She went to a window which was partially secured and, drawing the curtains, realized the school auditorium that was used as a shelter had sustained severe damage and those who were utilizing the shelter were now in peril.

The Alwyn Allison Richardson's shelter housed very few persons from the West End area. However, when the roof was torn apart by the storm, the rescue effort by the authorities was another matter. It was said that one of the occupants suffered from dementia and began to give his story of the trauma he experienced. He claimed he was on a journey from England and after landing in St. Martin on Air France, he took the ferry to Anguilla. The storm tossed the boat from every side for many hours and finally the waves were so high that the sea entered the boat, sinking it to the bottom of the ocean.

One of the ladies who tried to assist in the rescue effort thought he was suffering from post-traumatic stress disorder. However, she soon learned of his illness and dealt with him accordingly. The nearby residents gladly accepted those who were destitute. The gentleman with dementia was welcomed into a dwelling house and received excellent care. He was given a hot cup of coffee and breakfast. He remained in the house until the storm ended. It was not a difficult task for the lady of the house to exhibit such care as she was also caring for a relative who suffered from the same illness.

However, she had to be on the alert, as even her relative with dementia kept likening the storm to being on a ship that had been overtaken by the waves of the sea. At no point did they sleep during the storm. They were all fully alert and continued to speak about their delusions.

Finally, all were returned to their homes without injuries. It was very heroic of the residents of the area who braved the fierce winds of the storms in an effort to rescue those from the collapsed shelter in the West End school auditorium. The Anguillian spirit of benevolence was being demonstrated in the truest sense of the word.

CHAPTER XII

UNRELENTING PERSEVERANCE

After weathering many storms, my cousin Ursilla, at one hundred and four years old, must now brave another.

She was widowed at an early age, having to raise three children on her own during Anguilla's days of much hardship. Retrieving potable water from holes in rocks and tilling the soil that produced a little sweet potato, peas and corn was the order of survival. Fishing was easy during those days; it was not difficult for her to have her children sit on a rock while she took a metal two-gallon bucket and tried to scoop up fish that were in abundance at the shoreline. At times, the sea provided a harvest of fish for the natives; in the early mornings it was not uncommon to see fish on the shore struggling to get back into their habitat. Ursilla said, "I cannot recall life being hard, I saw it as being good, Lord, we helped each other in those good ole days."

As she gave me her discourse on Hurricane Irma, the Terrorist, I was very much awestruck and enthused by a statement she made. Sitting in her easy chair, she recounted, "Life is not hard cuz if you know the power of perseverance, no storm, no fire and no damn hard times could ever slow your progress. Corn-funji and fish was all we knew growing up and maybe that gave us the rebounding power when hit by disasters time after time."

Her house was built in two sections. She called one portion the "old part of the house," the other the "new part of the house." Whilst the Terrorist, Hurricane Irma, swept through the island and bore down on her house, she nestled herself in the old part of the house where she rested peacefully. She claimed that for one reason or another she felt the "old part of the house" was more sturdy and built with the resilience needed for winds of such magnitude.

Ursilla, due to her age, does not hear very well but her eyesight is like an eagle's. She wears her glasses for reading purposes on occasions but she can spot a moving object from a distance.

As the howling of the winds intensified she would mutter a prayer, "Lord, remember mercy." She recognized that her knees would not be able to take her quickly to the neighbor's house so she made sure her flashlight was close so she could hide herself in the bathroom should her room be endangered. She referred to her bathroom as her bunker.

Her caretaker was only a call away but to rely on her was useless. Actually, the caretaker drew strength from Ursilla. The gnashing of the caretaker's teeth with every pounding of the storm's winds against the house caused Ursilla to be more concerned about the caretaker than the storm.

Ursilla, having mobility issues, kept massaging her knees, as she wanted to get them in shape should she have to run to the neighbor's house. She kept reliving the many storms she had been through over her lifetime of one hundred and four years and was confident that whilst she may lose some earthly possessions, her life would be spared.

Whilst many used the radio and social media platforms as a guide to the required preparation for the storm, Ursilla knew the precautions all too well. One of the things she noted was the disappearance of the birds. She kept looking into the sky a day before the storm and noted blue skies without any birds. At that point she told her caretaker that this was going to be "one hell of a hurricane." However, she was mindful that if God could take care of the birds, he would take care of her.

When the door at the front of her house got blown in, she lifted her hands to the heavens and said, "Thank God." She was mindful that the good book says give thanks at all times.

Late in the afternoon, after the winds had subsided, she pulled herself from her bed, being guided by one or two birds that she noted in the sky through a crack in the window in her bedroom. At that point she realized the storm had passed. She gradually walked to her living room and peering through the dangling remains of her door her heart fainted at the destruction she observed.

In her mind she began to relive Hurricane Donna, which had devastated Anguilla around September 6th, 1960. She knew that Anguilla had very little infrastructure back then and it took quite a long time to rebuild; hence, she thought that Anguilla had so many more buildings, roads, water and electrical facilities now that the rebuilding would not be completed in her lifetime. To her surprise, she saw electricity and water restored island-wide within three months. After eight months of the passage of the storm, she claimed, "Cuz' we did damned good to bounce back so quick; ar you hear de hell."

Nature's Terrorist Hurricane Irma

CHAPTER XVIII

THE COLLAPSE OF ESSENTIAL SERVICES

All was going fine at Radio Anguilla, the Government of Anguilla-owned facility. It was purported that many persons were dialed in to the station, as it had direct links with the Disaster Preparedness Unit. The process was clear; The Disaster Preparedness Unit provided Radio Anguilla with updates on the storm.

In the wee hours of the morning the radio station received a call inquiring as to the passage of the hurricane; the person informed the station that it was evident that the storm had passed and there was no need to remain indoors. The radio announcer called the Disaster Preparedness Unit via her FLOW mobile telephone service and informed them of the caller's assertion. However, the Disaster Preparedness Unit cautioned the citizens to remain indoors securely as the brunt of the storm was imminent. The announcer hoped the caller took heed but couldn't be sure. Many called the station reporting the damage. Many were perplexed, disturbed, scared and angry; the announcer was placed in the position of bringing calm in this impending boisterous storm.

The young, nineteen-year-old radio announcer, Ms. Nisha Dupuis, told *The Guardian*, "I was in the studio when the winds started increasing around 1 a.m., but it really started picking up drastically about 2 a.m.

"By 4 a.m., the winds were so strong that the radio station's shutters were completely blown away. The men who were in the studio (a producer and a presenter) had to hold up a board in front of the window so that the pressure in the room would not get to the point where the window would explode. At this time, we had to keep on announcing on air and taking 911 calls."

She continued, "One woman who phoned in said the pole outside her house was sparking and she was afraid that it would catch fire. One man said he had a baby in the room with him and he was not sure what to do. He was helpless, saying: 'Help me, help me.' I told him to get into the bathroom – that was the advice we were given."

In her interview, Ms. Dupuis claimed, "The pressure in the studio was similar to that in an airplane. You had to keep unlocking your jaw; you kept opening your mouth to release the pressure. The walls were vibrating. We had to put a garbage bag over the door to protect it.

"Then the system went down and we went off air and I decided to share what was happening on Twitter.

"I got a voice message from my mother saying the hospital where she worked was flooding and the roof was being blown away and her voice was shaking so much. I called her and couldn't get a response. I was pacing the hallway trying to catch myself because I was so overwhelmed about what could have happened to my family, about the helplessness I was feeling when people were calling in with their emergencies and the tears they were crying.

"At one point I let out a yelp as there was a loud crash outside and I thought it was a projectile coming through the window.

"I was standing in front of an exposed window and, while there was someone with a board in front of the window, it was feeble. If something had decided to fly at that window, there was no way we would have lived."

My personal interview with Ms. Dupuis actually brought tears to my eyes as she relived the experience through words and expressions. After six months, the impact of this storm remained vivid.

As the day gave way to the evening on September 5th, 2017, the hospital maintenance team was certain that the equipment and the building was secured in accordance with their disaster preparedness plan. The health professionals who were required to work during the passage of the Terrorist, Hurricane Irma, gathered their family members who were under their care and secured them in certain areas of the hospital. This was strategically done to ensure their presence did not impede the smooth running of the organization.

All hunkered down with minimal fears of any serious damage to the infrastructure or equipment, but the staff soon realized the preparation was no match for the storm. The shutters used to secure the emergency room's glass windows began vibrating with much intensity; any possibility of adding to their strengthening was considered in vain and the shutters soon went flying from their positions, adding to the debris in the hospital's vicinity. Soon thereafter, the ferocious winds began tearing the glass louvres out en masse. At this point, the maintenance team broadened to include the health professionals who now had to engage in removing delicate equipment in an effort to avoid damages to it. The maintenance team had to create a makeshift emergency room, as the health professionals on the emergency team needed to be prepared to receive the injured who had been exposed to the fury of this Terrorist.

The maintenance team was very fearful of the security of the dialysis machine, which was housed in a shipping container external to the main hospital building. It was the team's view that one of the first objects that would crumble under the deadly forces of Hurricane Irma was this container. The island was lucky; the container with the dialysis equipment withstood the fierceness of the storm. When it was noted that it survived the storm, one of the medical practitioners exclaimed, "Miracles still happen today; the prayers of the saints have been felt."

However, the maternity ward and the female ward, which were quite close to each other, received the full wrath of the monster. The employees were confident the roof structure and design could withstand the fierce winds, as it had withstood a few storms before with minor damage. Little did they realize this Terrorist was determined to "throw down" every object in its path in record time, as its intention was to create a name for itself: "The worst storm mankind would have ever felt." An hour or two into the vibrating, the galvanized metal sheeting gradually gave in to its nemesis and like a leopard hunting its prey, Hurricane Irma tore that roof off with a vengeance.

Luckily, no babies were being delivered during that time. The female ward was now closed and the men's and women's wards became one. In the meantime, many continued to pray for the safety of the roof of the men's ward. The prayers were granted as that area received minimal damage.

The interior of the hospital was now exposed, with gaping holes in its roof, and the pediatric, maternity and female wards were notably roofless and exposed to the outside elements. The scene was likened to the bombing of a suicide squad. The damage was horrendous and this medical facility now had to function under difficult working conditions.

Immediately after the winds subsided, the hospital became inundated with the injured. Families drove as far as they could and then hand-carried the injured for care. Lacerations and wounds from broken glass windows and doors now had to be treated in the hospital's damaged surroundings. However, the medical crew worked feverishly to ensure the health care was balanced between the in-house patients and out-patient emergency area. The medical professionals worked extremely hard in ensuring the injured received adequate care in record time considering the condition under which they were forced to work.

Queen Elizabeth Hospital was completely de-faced and it was the popular view that attention must be given to this facility with urgency. For most of us, the restoration process was not fast enough. The Queen of the United Kingdom's name on this facility could not call for any quicker response.

The main police station, all the schools and many other government buildings remain in disrepair.

CHAPTER XIX

LANDMARKS CURRENTLY ETCHED IN OUR MEMORIES

The remains of the oldest church building on the island, Ebenezer Methodist Church, are seen in the photo. The church was built and opened on July 25th, 1830. Its interior was exposed to the elements by Hurricane Irma, the Terrorist. This building survived many previous storms with minor damages, but Hurricane Irma was relentless in its quest to challenge the resilience of God's people. However, this did not prevent their traditional Sunday morning gathering. The congregation was soon ready to rebuild as donations were made available from different sources.

The picture below shows when frozen meat items were distributed as relief food in the month of November, 2017. There was a forty-foot container of whole lamb legs, pork legs, whole chickens and other frozen meats. This was a great treat for many of the nationals.

The Digicel pole seen below fell across the main access road in the South Hill area, which prevented the free movement of traffic between the eastern and the western parts of the island.

The yard of the old Ebenezer Methodist Church down in The Valley was viewed as a safe haven for some of its parishioners' cars but this proved otherwise, as seen in the picture below. The owners were aghast at the condition of their vehicles. Hurricane Irma indeed was merciless and ruthless and bent on destroying any object that was in its path or even on its periphery.

Indeed, this structure was built to last. It resisted the ferocious winds of Hurricane Irma and truly defended the exceptionally excellent skill of its builder. The partial damage to its roof, scorches and bruises on the building are the marks to show that Hurricane Irma had certainly passed by. It was designed and built by indigenous Anguillians.

A young woman walks the street in bewilderment as she views the devastation to her village, "Down in The Valley."

Beach erosion at CuisinArt Golf Resort and Spa at Rendezvous Bay, resulting from the ravages of the Terrorist, Hurricane Irma. This beach is one of Anguilla's best.

It was ingenious of the architects of this structure to install the artificial dunes. The gabion baskets withstood the ocean's surges, preventing the buildings' foundations from being undermined by the tumultuous waves.

This car was lost, but was soon found sitting on the fence of a neighbor.

The Seventh Day Adventist parishioners in the Long Bay village were bereft at the destruction of their edifice by the Terrorist, Hurricane Irma. Some walls exploded and the church was reminiscent of a building that was shelled by a B-2 Spirit heavy stealth bomber aircraft.

The interior of the Seventh Day Adventist Church at Long Bay was left open to the outside elements. The devastation caused by this horrendous storm continues to be a mystery, but the parishioners gathered on Sabbath to give their God thanks for his love and tender mercies.

The elderly persons of our country always make it abundantly clear that our house is our sanctuary; it's a place of shelter. Indeed, it was painful to observe our roofs scattered in the main road.

CHAPTER XX

BEHIND EVERY DARK CLOUD

As a boy in my preteens I would accompany my grandmother to a village called "The Hughes," which borders west of South Hill village. My grandmother, Agatha Richardson of South Hill, was a broom maker. She would travel distances to gather thatch and sticks to make her brooms. I marveled at times looking at her stooping for hours in the back of her yard with her archaic broom-making machinery. She had a couple galvanized nails partially hammered into a tree similar to that of the Ficus benjamina tree, a machete and a small volcanic stone. My grandmother was what we call a "Stooper," as she would stoop for eight hours plying her daily trade. She would clean a stick by placing one end on the stone and, in a stooped position, using her small knife to peel the outer layer. Many of her friends would pass by and tease her, "Oh Mom Gats, the winds gonna topple you, my child." Her usual response was, "Well, my child, a bad wind never blows." She was indeed a positive lady.

At the Hughes Village, there were very few houses; however, surrounding these houses were pea trees, maize trees and sweet potato vines. The peas and maize trees grew extremely tall from the vantage of a child and it was difficult to identify any response to Granny calling behind them.

As Granny walked in this area in search of fiber to make her broom, it was usual to hear echoes from behind the trees, "Oh Gatty, how you do?" She had a very soothing voice to those who were dear to her heart, and she would respond, "My child, tings ain't looking de best but, ah, my child, behind every dark cloud is a silver lining."

As a ten-year-old boy I could never understand granny's maxim. I understood the "dark cloud" part, but the "silver lining" posed some difficulty to my comprehension. My grandmother used this phrase consistently. I vividly recall, as an eight-year-old boy, seeing a friend of my grandmother's, affectionately called Aunt Tayee, sitting on the balcony chatting away. Suddenly, there was a cry from one of Aunt Tayee's children that her hog had been found hanging from the chain that tethered it to its pen. My grandmother and Aunt Tayee ran to the pen, both crying for the loss of the pig. As children, we didn't understand the meaning of the tears. Through her tears, my grandmother hugged Aunt Tayee and stated, "Well, Fla, the hog dead, but always remember, behind every dark cloud is a silver lining."

The months following the storm were very difficult financially for our people and to a great extent affected us socially. Many damaged homes still remain in disrepair due to lack of funding for the homeowners. Whilst many have questioned the government's conscience in this regard, there are those who recognize it doesn't have the wherewithal to provide relief of any magnitude beyond duty-free concessions and the easing of the property tax. The Government is actually "financially broke."

A report entitled "Country Economic Review 2017 Anguilla" has painted a gloomy picture of our county in the immediate aftermath of the Terrorist, Hurricane Irma. It stated that the economy had contracted by approximately 3.5 percent, having performed robustly in the first half of 2017. Between the years of 2014 to 2016, the island experienced three uninterrupted years of economic growth. However, the damages and losses resulted from the storm totaled $880 million, with one casualty and many injuries. The productive sectors suffered 58.4 percent of the total damage; the social sectors 28.2 percent, and the infrastructure brought up the rear. In actuality the storm has given a crippling blow to our economic engine, tourism.

Nevertheless, much good resulted from the storm. Many would scoff or throw stones at the "Silver Lining" aspect of the maxim, as I did to my grandmother as a boy. Be that as it may, there were many government buildings, including schools, edifices and the police station, that were in bad shape before the storm and were demolished by it. Hotels that may have been poorly constructed were now in a good position to benefit from their insurance policies, whether self-insured or otherwise. Further, had there been no Hurricane Irma, there would not have been the heightened interest in extending the airport to accommodate international flights from the United States mainland or the United Kingdom.

The bravery and foresight of the current minister of infrastructure, the Honorable Curtis Richardson, was met with mixed emotions. He recognized the storm as a blessing rather than a curse. He exhorted everyone that the fate of the storm must now strengthen their faith in God, saying, "Behind every dark cloud is a silver lining." Whilst some of his political nemeses labeled him as "The Minister of Demolition," he fearlessly pressed ahead and through all the means at his disposal did not settle for repairs of many of the damaged government structures as suggested by the British authorities; but he continued the task of demolition, which was started by the Terrorist, Hurricane Irma.

He saw it as a means of replacing a structure with a model that met the current demands of the times. The Blowing Point terminal building was one of his fiercest battles. It was suggested that a temporary tent be erected at a cost of a few hundred thousand dollars, as the existing edifice required extensive repairs. In his disgust over the suggestion, words of obscenity like fire from a dragon's mouth filled the air. He maintained that to erect a tent for a few months would lead to years, that it was just a part of how the British government dispenses its remedies with "sugar-coated pills."

The removal of the secondary school from its existing location in The Valley had been contemplated over the years. Having two separate campuses in separate locations, Campus A and Campus B, under the same leadership seemingly was burdensome. Further, the population growth rendered Campus B a "concrete jungle," with little room for expansion in the immediate future. Some of the buildings had been erected at the inception of secondary education on Anguilla. The government's voice in lobbying for the required funding to mitigate some of these issues was weak.

However, Hurricane Irma's winds became the catalyst that opened the understanding of such donor agencies, particularly the British government. The people of Anguilla are now hopeful of a newer and more modern facility for their children to enjoy the type of hardware and software that meet global standards.

Most of the six public primary schools are now seeing reconstruction in action. Again, some of these buildings were in a decrepit condition prior to Hurricane Irma and finally succumbed to the storm's fierce winds.

In 2013, the government of Anguilla created a makeshift docking facility on Dutch St. Maarten to accommodate transit passengers to Anguilla. Intended to service the nearby Princess Juliana Airport, the dock was temporary in nature. Further, the actual berth facility, whilst usable by the sea shuttles, needed some significant adjustments requiring funding beyond the government's pocket. The building and the wharf were completely destroyed by Hurricane Irma. The tourist board, along with the minister, the Honorable Victor

Banks, and the parliamentary secretary, the Honorable Cardigan Connor, were adamant that they would provide a more solid structure with more appropriate docking facilities. Actually, the new area has now been realized and it's a mere thirty seconds away from Princess Juliana Airport. Reports of a much better facility have been recorded by guests who were familiar with the previous facility.

CuisinArt Golf Resort and Spa, had lost a significant portion of its market share over the years to newer resorts in the region. Like Cap Juluca, it sits on one of Anguilla's prime beaches and commenced business on December 20th, 1999, in the immediate aftermath of Hurricane Lenny, which flooded the island. It rivaled Cap Juluca, Anguilla's long-standing flagship resort, in every way, with the exception of its cuisine offering. As a member of the Leading Hotels of the World, it was strongly positioned among its competitive set for its service delivery, but fell short on its product offering, including its physical structure, fittings and furnishings. Whilst the ownership would have made some investments in the latter, it was not sufficient for its rebounding back into the market. However, the devastation from the Terrorist, Hurricane Irma, resulted in the ownership committing over $35,000,000 (US) to the rebuilding, renovating and restructuring of this facility.

Malliouhana Hotel, an Auberge property, had been open for a few years after it had been purchased by Adventurous Journeys Capital Partners (AJ Capital Partners) from the Roydon family. It had been suffering significant losses since being acquired due to certain infrastructural matters. Having received damages by Hurricane Irma, the hotel is currently seeking to correct such flaws, which would better position it in the marketplace.

Many other properties really saw Hurricane Irma as a blessing in disguise and used its devastation to their advantage.

The resilience of the Anguillian population and investors cannot be overstated. The pain and hurt from the storm have been felt by many, but the appeal to our innermost strength dominates, even though some continue to suffer from "Post Hurricane Stress and Trauma." And whilst the marks and scars of the devastation will forever be etched in our memory banks, we will not leave behind the lessons that have been learnt.

As a longtime resident said to me recently, "Chris, disasters, natural or unnatural, are always lurking around to attack your possessions and your health. What you would have spent your energies building for the succeeding generation can evaporate before your very eyes in a split second. It is left for us to learn that at some point in time the new must replace the old, by will or by force; and if you are caught sleeping you will die dreaming of the old."

We indeed face a new era in Anguilla's history. We are prepared to face the future having arisen from the ashes of despair and hopelessness with a new resolve that Anguilla is our home and we will make it a safe haven for all. With intestinal fortitude and an indomitable spirit, hand in hand, we will restore, revive and reestablish our nation. Who would have thought that the small island state of Anguilla would have had a young lady in the person of Dee Anne Kentish Rogers to be the first lady of color (black) to become Miss Universe Britain in 2018 in the aftermath of Hurricane Irma? Anguilla, after hosting the famous "John T Cycling Race" for almost twenty years, in 2018, had its first champion, nineteen-year-old Hasani Hennis from Blowing Point, Anguilla. Zanel Hughes, a world-class sprinter, and Shara Proctor, a world-class long jump athlete, both indigenous Anguillians, have stepped up their tenacity in the aftermath of Hurricane Irma and are making significant marks on the world stage. There are more victories we have garnered on regional and other fronts.

As a people, we have not only adopted the maxim, "Behind every dark cloud is a silver lining," but have learnt to relish excerpts from the songs of the late great Bob Marley, "…the hotter the battle the sweeter the victory," and Anguilla's very own musical genius Omarie Banks, "…just move on, by faith the battle's won."

Nature's Terrorist Hurricane Irma

BIBLIOGRAPHY

1. https://www.theguardian.com/world/2017/sep/13/boris-johnson-anguilla-absolutely-hellish-hurricane-irma

2. http://theanguillian.com/2017/10/CM-BANKS-WRITES-UK-MINISTER-LORD-AHMAD-UPDATING-AND-REQUESTING-ASSISTANCE-FOLLOWING-HURRICANE-IRMA/

3. https://www.theguardian.com/world/2017/sep/12/hurricane-irma-british-aid-derisory-caribbean-tax-havens

4. https://www.theguardian.com/commentisfree/2017/sep/12/hurricane-irma-british-territories-aid-anguilla

5. https://www.theguardian.com/world/2017/sep/09/britain-not-doing-enough-to-help-its-caribbean-territories

Nature's Terrorist Hurricane Irma

ABOUT THE AUTHOR

J. Christopher Richardson has had a long career in the operations of the hospitality industry, spanning some thirty years, during which he served at three of Anguilla's five acclaimed five-star resorts at the executive level. He is a public speaker, certified international trainer, and the founder and managing director of Rich Pearl Global Training Coaching & Consultancy Group. He holds a Bachelor of Science with honors from Chicago State University, Illinois (USA) and a Master of Business Administration from Durham School of Business (United Kingdom).

Chris, as he is affectionately called, enjoys honing leadership aptitude in people and is considered the ultimate extrovert. He has served on many statutory boards on Anguilla and has provided consultancy work for tertiary learning institutions locally and regionally. He is very vocal on the socioeconomic and political development of

the Caribbean region and advocates that a nation is as strong as its investment in its human capital.

Chris is an island boy, having been born in Sandy Point, St. Kitts. He migrated to Turks and Caicos Islands for a few years; thereafter, his family moved to Anguilla, the birthplace of his father. He is married to Sandra Richardson. The couple has three children and two grandchildren. He is an ardent man of faith and is a cultural relativist.